MW00906542

Warped Rods and Squeaky Reels

Also by Robert H. Jones, published by Horsdal & Schubart:

Tangled Lines and Patched Waders

Warped Rods and Squeaky Reels

Robert H. Jones

Horsdal & Schubart

Copyright © 1997 by Robert H. Jones

No part of this book may be reproduced or transmitted in any form by any means, electronic or mechanical, including photocopying and recording, or by any information storage and retrieval system, without written permission from the publisher, except for brief passages quoted by a reviewer in a newspaper or magazine.

Horsdal & Schubart Publishers Ltd.
Victoria, BC, Canada

We acknowledge the support of the Canada Council for the Arts for our publishing program.

Cover painting by Jim M. Wispinski, Victoria, BC.

This book is set in Lapidary 333 Book Text.

Printed and bound in Canada by Hignell Printing Limited, Winnipeg.

Canadian Cataloguing in Publication Data

Jones, Robert H., 1935-

Warped rods and squeaky reels

ISBN 0-920663-50-8

1. Fishing—Humor. 2. Fishing—Anecdotes. I. Title.
SH443.J66 1997   799.1'02'07   C97-910071-2

Printed and bound in Canada

DEDICATION

For Vera, my Prairie Belle

CONTENTS

§ FOUR: PERIPHERAL VISIONS

§ FIVE: MORE ONTARIO MEMORIES

§ SIX: THE TRAVELLING ANGLER

INTRODUCTION

Perhaps this will explain why the stories which follow bounce around so much: Four years after leaving school at age 14 to work in various remote logging and sawmill camps throughout southern British Columbia, I joined the First Regiment, Royal Canadian Horse Artillery. After a three-year hitch I returned to B.C. for a few months, then re-enlisted in the Royal Canadian Air Force. In all, my 27-year military career provided opportunities to visit or live in locations which had much to offer an outdoor enthusiast who was hung up on fishing, and who eventually found equal delight in writing about his exploits. This delightful situation has continued since I became a full-time freelancer in 1980. My previous book, *Tangled Lines and Patched Waders*, introduced readers to many of the folks I met during my travels throughout B.C. and Ontario — some wonderful, some wacky, and some who were downright weird. This book is simply a continuation which covers a much wider range of geography, but the types of characters met along the way remain in basically the same categories.

Finally, as stated in my introduction to *Tangled Lines and Patched Waders*, I still maintain that the following holds true: Fishing rods are the world's greatest equalizers. They can span the years between childhood and old age, knock down walls of prejudice, and totally eradicate class barriers. It's too bad more politicians and senior bureaucrats don't fish.

§ ONE
WHEN I WAS A YOUNG MAN ...

POACHERS

Like most farm boys living in British Columbia's Fraser Valley, my chums and I got into our share of mischief, but it was mostly pretty tame stuff like playing hooky or swiping apples from old farmer Hairygun's orchard. Our most dastardly sin was poaching steelhead smolts and cutthroat trout from the Salmon River. We were constantly reminded that fishing wasn't allowed, but to us, at seven or eight years of age, having a stream flowing through our rural neighbourhood and not being able to fish in it was simply incomprehensible.

Although our parents hardly condoned our criminal activities, whatever we caught always made it to the tables in our respective homes, for with money scarce during those postwar years, all contributions were gratefully received. The truth is, our fathers seldom had much to say on the subject, but our mothers often prophesied that the game warden would catch us and we would all end up in reform school until we were at least 21 years old. Maybe longer. This blatant scare tactic didn't stop us from fishing, but it certainly ruined what could have been otherwise idyllic times.

Hairygun's farm bordered one side of the river, and most of it was an open field where he kept several head of dangerously demented cattle, including a bull of truly massive size that possessed sharp horns and a nasty temper. Fortunately, the opposite shoreline consisted of dense forest and a sizable cedar swamp, making it much better suited for our clandestine activities. Never mind that we feared it was crawling with ravenous grizzly bears, vicious cougars, sharp-fanged wolverines, hideous crocodiles and horrific tarantula spiders as large as basketballs — getting torn limb from limb and eaten alive was nothing compared to being apprehended by the game warden, and then incarcerated in reform school. We knew that crocodiles and tarantulas were not native to B.C., but had heard all about zoo animals and pets escaping from captivity, most of which we were certain had taken up residence in our swamp.

It was amazing how we three happy, carefree youths were suddenly turned into furtive, paranoid criminals by simply stepping off the gravel road and taking handlines out of our pockets. We would fearfully search our surroundings, first for the game warden, then wild animals. We often heard vague sounds, but never quite saw what made them. One or the other of us often detected slight, fleeting movements among the trees, but we never all saw the same thing at the same time. With three of us scanning our gloomy, dangerous surroundings, we usually found ourselves totally surrounded by ... things.

Choking down our fear, we used whispered commands and hand signals to deploy ourselves along the river bank, then cautiously lowered our worm-baited hooks into the dark, swirling water, ever alert so as not to present a target for lurking crocodiles. Tense as we were, the slightest unidentified sound abruptly sent us scurrying frantically in several directions at once. Never mind that it was only a dead branch clattering to the ground, the guttural muttering of a raven, or the scratching of a red squirrel scampering up a tree — hasty, panic-stricken departures were made in whichever direction we happened to be facing at the time. As the river was often in our direct line of travel, more often than not we arrived home thoroughly drenched.

On one memorable occasion Norman Dewflower was walking down the trail when Curly Wallace coughed. Once. A single, loud, hollow-sounding bronchial bark. Immediately galvanized into action,

Norm was just getting up a good head of steam when he raced headlong into a large alder tree, knocking himself senseless. A few minutes later, when I cautiously returned from my own cross-country excursion through the swamp and halfway across a four-acre field of sugar beets, Curly said it was really amazing how Norm's legs kept pumping until he was dug down between the tree roots almost to his knees. Norm's nose was bent a bit to one side and his eyes stayed more or less crossed for almost an hour, but he seemed okay except for being a bit vague and confused about who he was and where he lived.

Another time, while we were fishing near the bridge, a passing truck backfired. Now the river being only 20 feet wide where Curly was fishing, he easily cleared it in a standing broad jump and was well on his way toward running the one-minute mile when he encountered Hairygun's barbed-wire fence. It stretched almost to the breaking point before catapulting him halfway back across the river, removing the entire front of his shirt along with assorted pieces of hide in the process.

At the truck's explosive backfire, Norman streaked off down-stream in a straight, blessedly treeless line before encountering an extremely large cow patty dead centre in the trail. He tried to stop, but was travelling so fast that his feet skidded, then shot out from under him. From the looks of Norm's pants, sweater and hair, not much of that bovine deposit was left on the ground when he finally got up.

My friends were lucky. When my own legs became a blur of motion, a large blackberry patch loomed on my escape route, and I actually made it halfway across. Which didn't hurt nearly as much as trying to extricate myself from that dense tangle of sharp thorns.

A FEAST OF FISH

I watched silently from the warm folds of my down-filled sleeping bag as Bert Anderson squatted in front of the stove, building a fire by dim, flickering candlelight. In a matter of minutes the tiny stove, built from a rectangular, five-gallon oil can, would heat our single, windowless cabin.

The tiny building was identical to several others located along Bert's trap line: about 10 feet long, six wide, and eight feet high at the ridge. Small and cramped, yet comfortable and easy to heat — a necessary trait when we arrived cold and hungry after a day of slogging through the snow. It was constructed entirely from red cedar: large-diameter heavy log walls, smaller ones as rafters, split-plank gables, and overlapping shakes on the roof. Inside was a low bunk bed, and a narrow shelf that encircled the room — all of split cedar that had been shaved smooth with a draw knife.

The fire to his liking, Bert stood up, stretched, and groaned in ecstasy as joints cracked and muscles loosened. He looked funny in his long, baggy, woollen underwear, his hair tousled, and his unlit, crooked-stemmed pipe already gripped in his teeth. "C'mon young feller," he said, peering owlishly over the black rims of his glasses. "It's daylight in the swamp. If you sleep all day we'll never make it to Rainbow Crick by dark."

I groaned at thoughts of the trip facing us, but unzipped my bag and rolled out over Bert's bag to the bunk's edge. As I pulled heavy wool stockings over my bare feet, Bert, now clad in pants, shirt and boots, pushed the wooden hatch from the small, square entrance that served as a doorway. The room was flooded with bright, blinding light, and a blast of cold air hurried my getting dressed.

Our morning meal was identical to those of the previous six days: a heaping plate of boiled rolled oats that was smeared with butter then seasoned with salt and pepper, a fist-sized chunk of cold bannock liberally coated with strawberry jam, and black coffee which Bert claimed was "strong enough to make a Scandahoovian logger twitchy." Not terribly appetizing, but palatable — and substantial enough to keep us going until nightfall with only a midday piece of bannock to chew on. Which, considering I was a lanky 15-year-old with a seemingly insatiable appetite, said quite a bit about Bert's choice of trail food. His credo was: If it don't weigh much, stays down and sticks to your ribs, it's good trail grub.

Cleaning up the diminutive cabin was quick. The short crosscut saw — rusty, but newly sharpened and oiled upon our arrival — was hung from a spike by the entrance. Sawn blocks of dry larch were stacked under the overhanging roof, then a small supply of split firewood and cedar kindling was stowed under the bunk. The stove and pipes were dismantled and cleaned, and the chimney hole in the roof plugged with a tapered peg of cedar that had been shaped to provide a tight fit.

Two tin plates and enamel mugs, a sheet-metal frying pan, and two half-gallon tin cans went with us. Bert knew from experience it was better to carry the extra weight and ensure having utensils on hand, than depend on the honesty of visitors who appeared during the fishing and hunting seasons. Even in the early 1950s, inconsiderate slobs wandered around and burnt up firewood without replacing it; ate dehydrated rations left as emergency stock; stole whatever struck their fancy; and left the entrance hatches off cabins so what they didn't plunder could be worked over thoroughly by rodents, porcupines or bears.

Our cleanup complete, we donned bearpaw snowshoes and helped each other into the harness of our heavy pack boards. A few weeks earlier I had sat in Bert's one-roomed house at Sugar Lake, watching as he fashioned my snowshoes from red cedar saplings and rawhide. Each piece of the frames was steamed over a basin filled with boiling water, which eventually made it pliant. He started with the long pieces first. Once each was supple enough, Bert gripped it by the ends, then sat on a chair, centred the wood against his knees and pulled the ends toward him. As the wood cooled and became stiffer, it received further steaming. The end results were two long, U-shaped pieces that formed the wide toe and body of each snowshoe. To shape the two short pieces forming the narrow tails of the snowshoes, Bert used only one knee around which to bend the wood.

The joints were tapered and shaped with a sharp knife, then the long and short U-shaped pieces were bound tightly together with wet strips of rawhide — no nails or screws. The rawhide webbing was skilfully laced and woven around the frames in a wide, three-inch mesh. The finished product had no resemblance to sleek commercially-made snowshoes, but they outperformed them in the wet snow common in British Columbia's Monashee Mountains. The short, tailless frames made it easy to walk up and down steep trails, and the open weave prevented a heavy, wearying build-up of snow atop the webs.

Our packs were lighter than on the trip in — less the weight of the stove, pipes, and a week's supply of food. We weren't weighed down with skins, either, for the pickings had been slim: five marten, one mink, and a dozen or so ermine.

Once we were on the trail, clouds obscured the sun, dulling the morning light. Stately evergreens, their branches laden and bent with cloaks of heavy snow, appeared sombre, almost black — like a monochrome painting rendered on stark white canvas. The only sounds were those of our bearpaws lifting, advancing and descending at the rhythmic pace set by my companion; the measured, even breathing associated with steady walking; the occasional snuffling of a runny nose; the muted thump of Bert's walking staff jarring snow from overhanging branches.

A tough, wiry man, Bert was trail-wise and could set a pace capable of eating up distance at a good rate without pushing either of us to our limit of endurance. This was natural, I suppose, considering it had been his livelihood for most winters during his adult life — except for a couple. Bert had served as an infantryman during the Second World War, but not for long. His military career came to an abrupt halt on an Italian beachhead as he waded ashore from the landing craft. Scarcely a year after donning his khaki uniform, he was home on Canadian soil with a mutilated and shortened leg, a partial disability pension, and authorization entitling him to two pairs of custom-made, orthopaedic boots per year. He had stoically picked up the pieces of his disrupted life by working as a boom man at a small sawmill on Sugar Lake during the open-water season, and trapping during the winter months. "Some people figure I had a bad break," Bert once remarked, "but I was a damned sight luckier than a lot of guys who hit the beach that day."

We had worked together on the booming grounds the previous summer and fall, my second year out of school, and the relationship that formed was part teacher and pupil, part older and younger brother. When winter weather finally closed the mill, Bert reluctantly agreed to take me along on his trap line. However, after trial jaunts on a couple of his short, easily handled spur lines, he was sure enough of my stamina and ability with snowshoes to attempt this somewhat longer trip.

Our trek down the valley was uneventful. Not even a grouse presented itself as a target for Bert's .22 Colt Woodsman pistol, so it looked like beans and bannock for supper. Our destination was the cabin at Rainbow Creek, little more than a half-day jaunt. We could have started earlier in the day and made it through to Bert's Land Rover, parked at the trail-head beside the upper Shuswap River, but there was no rush to get back. The trail was mostly downhill, and eventually descended along the valley's bottom to Rainbow Creek. Although the creek was hidden beneath a deep mantle of snow, the chuckling, bell-like tinkle of its rushing water was clearly audible. Occasionally we passed abstract-shaped openings where we could see the creek. At one of them, Bert suddenly stopped and stared down into a shallow stretch of exposed water. "Would you look at that!" he exclaimed.

I shuffled up beside him and looked where his mittened hand pointed. It took a while for my eyes to adjust from white snow to the mosaic of rocks and pebbles below. Finally, flickers of movement revealed several small fish weaving back and forth in the current. "Trout?" I asked.

"Yep. Dwarf rainbows. They only get about eight inches long, even when they're fully grown. I've caught 'em here when I was prospectin'. Sweetest damned eatin' in the world."

"We got anything to catch 'em with?" I asked, my taste buds going into high gear at the thought of fresh trout to augment the beans for our final supper on the trail.

"Might be somethin' at the cabin. We're only 10 minutes away, so you'll have lots of time to come back before it gets dark."

At the cabin we used our snowshoes as shovels to clear away newly-fallen snow from the entrance and wood pile. As Bert set up the stove, I dusted off a few blocks of wood and split a supply to replace what would be burnt during our short stay. This chore completed, I untied the billy cans from the side of my pack, slipped into my bearpaws, then went for water from the creek. I dipped the water by tying a four-foot-long, leather boot lace to the end of my walking staff, then tying a can to the opposite end of the lace and lowering it into the current.

When I returned to the cabin, Bert said, "Here. Just what the doctor ordered." I groaned when he handed me a huge, No. 3/0 bronzed Mustad hook.

"Haven't you got anything else?" I asked.

"Yep, two more — both the same size."

I sat dejectedly on the bunk and studied the hook for a few moments, thoughts of trout for supper rapidly dwindling. "Why don't you heat it up," said Bert, "and try making it smaller?"

I thought the situation over, then forced the hook eye into the split end of a piece of kindling. Holding the bend of the hook over the candle flame, I watched it heat to cherry red. After allowing it to cool, I used my fork tines to straighten the now malleable wire, then recurved it into a rather horrible-looking contraption with a quarter-inch gap and a two-inch-long shank. I held it up for inspection. Bert studied my finished product and pronounced, "Well, it ain't much to look at, but those fish probably won't know the difference."

While I was busy with the fishhook, Bert dug into his pack and produced six feet of heavy, black linen thread. Tied to the boot lace, it gave me 10 feet of line.

"Got any bacon left for bait?" I asked while knotting my hook to the thread.

"Yep, a little piece. How much you want?"

"Not much. Just a thin slice of fat."

"Well, don't throw away whatever you don't use — we can always toss it in with the beans if you don't catch anything."

While retracing our steps upstream, I scouted for a suitable rod. Since it was evergreen country, small deciduous trees fared poorly in the heavily-shaded, rocky terrain. Those managing to eke out a precarious existence were buried deep in the snow, mostly out of sight except for an occasional tip. I settled on a slender branch of red cedar. Trimming it to relative smoothness created a rod about the length and thickness of a pool cue, and about as flexible. It already had an acute bow from supporting a load of heavy snow.

Arriving at the pool, I sliced off a greasy segment of bacon fat and threaded it over the hook's barb. The bend and shank were totally exposed, but I didn't think those unsophisticated little trout would mind. I was right. My bait no sooner hit the water when a fish had it. It was immediately lifted and swung over the snowbank, unhooked, then tossed onto the packed trail behind me.

It took longer than I anticipated to haul out the dozen trout I wanted for supper, for several shook free and dropped off my crude hook before I could lift them from the water. By the time I reached my quota, my exposed fingers were cold and numb. Tugging off my woollen tuque, I turned it inside out and scooped the fish into my makeshift bag. My fingers were too stiff to untie the leather thong from the rod's end, so I simply snapped the tip off the branch and rolled the line around it.

Bert was sitting by the open entrance, sipping a mug of tea when I arrived. His face broke into a wide grin when he saw my catch. "Hell! You didn't do bad at all. Get in here and thaw out while I clean 'em. Just look at 'em — what the good Lord didn't give 'em in size, He sure made up for in looks."

Compared to their larger cousins in Sugar Lake, each was a beautifully marked miniature: a heavily spotted body and dorsal fin, the distinct lateral band of crimson from gill covers to tail superimposed with bluish-grey parr marks. Dwarf rainbows confined in small streams retain their parr marks throughout adulthood.

As I sat on the bunk, warming from the stove's heat and a lip-blistering mug of black tea, Bert cleaned the trout, dusted them with flour and salt, then fried them quickly in a bath of bacon grease until they were a crispy, golden brown. Pure ambrosia! As he had stated earlier in the day: "... sweetest damned eatin' in the world."

That night, we slept as only people can who have had a hard day of strenuous exercise and a full, satisfying meal. The following morning, as Bert ministered to the rolled oats and coffee, I untied my impromptu fishing line and coiled it back into a leather boot lace and a length of linen sewing thread. Not knowing what to do with the hook, I simply reached over and buried its point in the wall beside me.

* * * *

During the next five years, I made it back to Rainbow Lake three times: The following winter trapping with Bert, and twice while I was on leave from the army, when I hiked in to fish for the lake's husky rainbow trout. We didn't use the Rainbow Creek cabin during my last trip on the trap line, but on both fishing trips I stopped long enough on the way in to pull the hatch from its entrance and peer into the gloomy interior. Both times I noticed that my hook was in the same spot. The last time was in 1955, so I have no idea whether or not the cabin still exists.

If I ever hike back up that trail and discover the cabin is still standing, I'll pull the hatch out and take a peek. Only this time, on the off chance that my old misshapen hook is still there, I'll pluck it free and place it carefully in my wallet. Then I'll replace it with three or four smaller hooks, ones much more suitable for catching dwarf rainbows, and a small coil of monofilament so the hungry traveller won't have to use a boot lace and linen thread for line. Bert Anderson would probably like that touch.

WADING

Across the channel, perhaps 20 yards away, a road angled away from the river to where my van was parked. The water depth and speed looked borderline for wading, but the alternative was walking 300 yards downstream to the next shallows, then either beating my way cross-country through a dense cedar swamp toward my van, or hiking 300 yards back upstream to the road.

I studied the bottom through my polarized glasses, hitched up my chest waders, then started across, quartering upstream toward a scattering of large boulders in mid-channel. Things got hairy when it proved deeper than I'd estimated, which found me up on tiptoe, fully expecting water to cascade in over my wader tops. As it worked out, Fate was kind, for I reached the lee of the first boulder with at least a quarter inch of freeboard to spare. With the current's force disrupted, it was easy going from there on.

I clambered up the steep gravel bank, intending to wait for Marcel and point out the easy crossing downstream. However, when I turned to face the river, there he was, standing almost in midstream, studying the water to determine his next move. I was impressed, for it was only his second time out steelheading and his experience at wading was limited. What really got me was how casual he seemed, for he was whistling away like a neoprene-clad canary. "Go straight upstream," I said. "Get in that slack water behind those big rocks and you'll be okay."

Marcel nodded. As he turned to face upstream, his body presented a wider silhouette to the current, which promptly caused him to wash downstream a couple of feet. He managed to retain his balance, then slowly inched upstream, side-stepping until he was in line to wade toward the boulders. He obviously felt in total control, for he kept right on whistling. Not much of a tune, but loud. When he finally crawled up the bank and stood beside me, I shook my head in wonder and said, "Pretty nice wading for a guy who hasn't done much. And chirping away like a canary the whole while."

"I always whistle when I'm nervous," Marcel replied tersely through clenched teeth.

"Nervous?"

"Extremely. Scared, really scared. No — terrified. All I could think about was that I'd quit smoking for nothing."

* * * *

River fishing and wading are an accepted fact of life for most anglers. While few can probably remember the first time they tried it, I can — vividly. I was just shy of my seventh birthday when my parents moved from Vancouver to a farm beside the Salmon River in the Fraser Valley. Until then my fishing had been confined to catching occasional bullheads from a pond in Memorial Park, so thoughts of fishing the small stream were pretty exciting. Although fishing was not permitted in the river, Father figured I would not prove much of a threat to whatever was swimming around in it. He rigged me up with a length of twisted linen line wrapped around a simple wooden frame, a lead sinker, and a large japanned hook, upon which I skewered a worm.

My first expedition ended downstream from the Otter Road bridge, where a fallen tree spanned the stream. I worked my way out about midway over the channel, sat down and lowered my hook. A minute or so later I suddenly felt something moving at the end of my line. I tugged up sharply, whereupon a huge, man-eating shark swirled on the surface, turned and raced downstream. My line tightened in an instant, then, too scared to even scream, I was jerked forward off my perch. The water below was well over my head, but I waded to shore so quickly I stayed dry above my waist.

Okay, so it was really a chinook salmon I had accidentally snagged, probably by a fin. But to a brand-new, fresh-from-the-city, not quite seven-year-old, it sure looked like a man-eating shark.

Despite my initial scare, I kept fishing. Over the years since, I have progressed from wading wet in running shoes, to wearing thigh waders, hip waders, then chest waders; and from cleated rubber soles to felts, and more recently to iron-caulked felts. Heavy rubber and canvas waders have evolved into tough, lightweight, long-wearing models, but while my waders have improved dramatically, I can't say the same for the "wadee." Despite all these advances, I still find myself wading wet on occasion.

There was a period when I considered myself quite a hotshot at wading the type of fast water sensible anglers shun. It provided an adrenalin rush similar to throwing myself out of completely serviceable military airplanes with a parachute, and a tremendous sense of satisfaction when I pulled off some particularly frightening wading without wiping out. The positive result of these foolish excursions was that I often found myself in good fishing situations that were denied my less mentally deranged companions. However, whenever I started getting visions of grandeur about my wading prowess, something would usually happen to jar me back to reality. Like during the early 1960s, when I set out with Mark Featherstonehaugh and General Sir Charles Loewen to fish steelhead on the Tsolum River, near Courtenay. We found the river higher than expected, and as was often the case, the opposite bank appeared to offer the best opportunities. I steeled my nerves and said, "I'm going across." I didn't bother asking my companions if they were interested in accompanying me, for both were in their sixties.

The torrent was every bit as tough as I envisioned, and got worse with each step. Each inch forward cost two or three inches downstream. The problem with wading beyond your ability is that it's virtually impossible to turn around and retreat without losing your footing and balance. Entirely. To say nothing about the embarrassment of admitting defeat in front of an audience. About the time I decided the current's pummelling force would sweep me downstream, I sensed a slight decrease in the pressure, then felt the bottom coming up. I was safe. Reaching some waist-deep slack water, I heaved a ragged sigh of relief and turned — almost whacking Mark in the face with my rod tip. He ducked, mumbling thickly as crumbs sprayed from his lips, "Bit swift, eh Charles?"

"Yes," mumbled the general in reply, "a bit." He finished chewing, swallowed, then said more clearly, "Nothing like fishing those mountain torrents in India for mahseer, though."

Not only had they waded across right behind me, they had done so while calmly munching a shared egg-salad sandwich.

* * * *

When John Humphries visits from Nova Scotia, we usually end up rehashing our fishing experiences from the mid-1960s. John's favourite yarn relates to our last trip together on the Oyster River prior to his posting to No. 4 Fighter Wing in Baden-Soellingen, Germany ....

It was late in the season, so we decided to try the upper river, about four miles west of the Island Highway. After negotiating a dirt track that branched from the Iron River Logging road, I parked right beside the river. John elected to fish downstream, so I headed up. The fish proved few and far between, but it was a warm spring day, and each bend revealed a few more likely-looking prospects. It took me all afternoon to cover two miles of water, then I retraced my steps downstream.

It was dusk when I sloshed around the last bend to see John sitting on the hood of my station wagon, smoking a cigarette. A deep pool ran straight toward him, then almost at his feet it veered sharply to the right. As I waded knee-deep along the edge of a sloping rock shelf, John raised his hand and waved. "How'd you make out?" he asked.

At precisely that moment, my foot landed on a slick patch of algae and shot sideways. I flailed my rod onto the water and managed to catch my balance — for all the good it did. Still standing upright, I slid slowly down the sloping shelf, then finally toppled sideways and disappeared. But not for long. I promptly stood up, now in the centre of the channel, with only my head and shoulders clearing the water. "Four," I replied, reaching for my hat, which had floated off my head. "How 'bout you?"

John stared at me for a few moments, then slowly exhaled a plume of smoke. "Six. Four of 'em were kelts, though."

I continued wading through the deep water toward him, the water supporting my body as the slow current aided me along. John slid off his perch and picked his way carefully down the rocky bank to meet me at the water's edge. After handing him my rod and fishing vest, I shrugged out of my suspenders. John extended his hand, then helped haul me up the bank as my water-filled waders emptied and collapsed down around my legs.

Once on level ground, I removed my waders and sloshed soggily to my vehicle, where a complete change of dry clothes was always stored in anticipation of such events. Throughout this entire period I expected John to start laughing and needling me, as I most certainly would have had our roles been reversed. However, he remained strangely quiet while I peeled out of my clothes, gave myself a cursory towelling, then dressed again.

It was a 20-minute drive out to the Island Highway, and during that whole time John hardly spoke a word. Then, the moment we hit asphalt, he suddenly threw back his head and roared with loud, hysterical laughter. "Haw-aw-aw!... That was the funniest-looking thing I've ever seen!" he bellowed. "You-hoo-hoo looked like a submarine going down!... haw-aw-aw!... and like 'The Creature From the Black Lagoon' coming back up."

"Well, I'm really glad I brightened up your day," I said evenly when he finally calmed down to what sounded like a terminal case of the dry heaves. "But why, pray tell, this delayed reaction in bringing it to my attention?"

This triggered another wave of uncontrollable braying. When it subsided, John breathed deeply to steady himself, then replied,

"Because now if you get mad and kick me out of the car, I can hitch-hike without having to walk all the way out to the highway." Then he started laughing again — nonstop — all the way home.

§TWO
MEMORIES AND MUSINGS

TALL TALES

Throughout the years, fishing lore has been liberally spiced with yarns of gigantic fish possessing monumental eating habits. Some are out-and-out myths, but others — hard as they are to believe — often turn out to be factual. One of the most famous fish stories dates back to 1497, when the skeleton of a huge pike was displayed at Mannheim Cathedral, in the German province of Wurttemburg. Known as the "Emperor's Pike," the impressive trophy measured 19 feet long, and was said to have weighed 550 pounds when caught. It was not until the 19th century that a sceptic pointed out most of the gigantic fish's length was constructed from the mid-sections of several different pike. Alas, the Emperor's Pike has since been known as the "Mannheim Hoax."

With a fish story like that to live up to, it is little wonder that European folklore abounds with tales of monstrous pike — all much larger than the German fish, of course. Some are said to have dragged screaming swimmers to their watery graves, others gobbled down full-grown swans as appetizers, and a few even grabbed mules, horses and other livestock by their respective snouts while they drank, then tried dragging them into the water.

Almost all of these leviathans were supposedly hooked by anglers, but none were ever landed. It appears that even back then, the big ones always got away.

Periodically, tales appear in various magazines and newspapers of man-eating fish in Iliamna Lake on the Alaska Peninsula. Originally, these stories involved hapless travellers having their kayaks and umiaks swamped, then ending up as snacks for giant fish said to lurk in the lake's mysterious depths. Handed down through generations of native people, this legend continues, with disappearances on the big lake still attributed to the gigantic creatures supposedly dwelling there. Adding fuel to these stories are occasional reports by aircraft pilots of sighting huge "marine creatures" cruising Iliamna's waters. Hmm ... anyone for swimming?

The following tale was related to me a few years ago by a friend who had recently returned from a fishing trip in Northern Ontario. "The other guys were hot and heavy into a card game, so I decide to go out in the canoe. I'm paddling along, trolling a big silver spoon, when all of a sudden I get one hell of a strike. I throw the paddle down and grab for the rod just as it's going over the side, and just in time to see a big pike — 20 pounds at least — break water behind the canoe. Now the biggest fish we'd seen so far was only about half that size, so I immediately get visions of winning the pool with that baby — if I got it in.

"Well, that big old momma is really giving me a tussle, when all of a sudden the fight just stops and there's nothing but dead weight on the end of my line. I figure maybe she's fouled in a weed bed or something, so I grab the paddle and start back towards her — hanging onto the rod with one hand and paddling with the other. I'm only about a rod-length away from the fish when I spot it about four feet down from the surface — crossways in the mouth of the biggest goddam pike I've ever seen! Or heard of! So I did what any red-blooded Canadian fisherman would do under the same circumstances — I cut the line and got the hell out of there as fast as I could make that canoe go. Now before you go asking me why I'd do such a thing, let me explain that there was only about two feet of my fish showing — one foot on each side of that big one's yap."

"You know," he finished off dreamily, reaching for yet another dram of Ye Olde Kidney Convulser, "if they ever put a half-decent road into that place, I might try trailering in a 25-foot boat and take another go at that monster. But in the meantime I ain't going nowhere near that place."

* * * *

When it comes to the eating habits of some of the larger, more voracious fish, fact is never far removed from fiction. Considering the vast assortment of furry and feathered creatures paddling about on the surfaces of creeks, rivers and lakes — whether on purpose or by accident — it is little wonder that the finned denizens swimming around below have learned to welcome these sources of protein to their diet.

There are many documented cases of large pike and muskies making meals of full-grown ducks. Like the time Bruce Miller, a fishing guide from Waubaushene, Ontario, was watching a half-dozen mallards puddling about the edge of a weed bed one fall day, when a sudden commotion scattered them in noisy flight. However, one seemed anchored to the spot despite flapping its wings mightily in a futile attempt to get airborne. The cause of its distress materialized as the frantically squawking duck disappeared below the surface, then the broad tail of a large pike flipped slowly into the air.

The wily young guide made a mental note of the area and returned the next day. Although he took an 18½-pounder in the vicinity, Bruce doubted that it was the duck-eater. "I didn't find anything in its stomach resembling bones or feathers — and I don't think it would digest them that fast. Besides, the tail of the fish I saw looked to be at least half-again as big as the one we got."

My first recollection of using other than standard baits goes back to the early 1950s in the North Okanagan. A large bull trout had eluded all attempts to dredge him from his hole in the Shuswap River, a few miles below Sugar Lake. One day a young sawmill worker from Saskatchewan gave the cagey old fish exactly what he had been waiting for — a freshly killed pocket gopher. At 15 pounds that bull trout was hardly a record, but he was big for the Shuswap. It also gave several local anglers an acute case of terminal jealousy to think that a "stubble-jumper" had bested them on their own turf.

The fly-fishing fraternity sings loud praises for the wisdom and wile of brown trout, and justly so. Successful anglers must be skilled to present their dainty flies with the caution and subtlety necessary to deceive these worthy fish. However, mounted specimens that cause palpitation of the heart among anglers are usually caught on lures or bait. And more than a few old-time river anglers swear up and down that nothing beats a freshly-killed mouse when it comes to tempting lunker browns.

Bass are also notorious opportunists when it comes to taking advantage of whatever tidbit is made available. A few years ago, while fishing the Rideau River near Ottawa, I spotted a nestling bird floundering about in the water upstream from my canoe. Apparently it had fallen or been pushed from the nest, a fairly common occurrence according to my bird-watching friends. As the struggling bird swept downstream toward me, I mentally debated whether to attempt a futile rescue, for I had no idea where its nest was, or to simply let it drown. The decision was suddenly taken from my hands by the appearance of a hefty smallmouth bass. The fish, which looked to be all of five pounds, simply slurped that little pinfeathered bird down as though it were a large fly. I'm not sure what species the baby bird was, but prefer to think it was a pigeon. Having fished under numerous bridges throughout my life, I don't harbour any great love for those feathered feces-flingers, so the more of them that end up feeding fish, the better. The point is that eating habits such as this might be the basis for future tall tales. After all, fish are known to gain a few inches or pounds with each telling, so whatever it is they happen to eat is bound to do the same.

THE FOAMING DOCTOR

It happens every year about the middle of the winter steelhead season, usually in late February or early March: the first signs of skunk cabbage. As each hooded, cobra-shaped yellow leaf and spadix thrusts from the wet earth, one of British Columbia's most beautiful harbingers of spring is revealed, along with the distinct, pungent odour of skunk — a small price to pay for such a colourful display.

Their appearance reminds me of Ken "Doc" Hampson's first visit to Vancouver Island during the mid-1960s. As we hiked the Browns River trail near Courtenay, Doc was clearly smitten with our surroundings. "I can't get over it," he marvelled. "Everything is so lush and green — it's almost sub-tropical."

Thick, spongy moss carpeted the forest floor beneath our feet, and while a dense canopy of evergreens blocked most of the early May sunlight there was no shortage of undergrowth. Waxy green salal, holly-like Oregon grape, huckleberry bushes clinging to rotting stumps, spiky clusters of fern, flowering salmonberry bushes, and throughout the shadowed glade, the last colourful remnants of trilliums showing white, pink and magenta. As we approached a low, swampy area, Doc suddenly stopped and asked, "What's that beautiful green plant with the huge leaves?"

"Skunk cabbage," I replied. "They grow all through this area. When they first come up in the spring they're bright yellow, then, as they grow larger and mature, they go through a lime green phase to dark green."

"So that's skunk cabbage. I've heard of them, but I've never seen one before. Why such a derogatory name for such a pretty plant?"

"Come around in early spring and you'll find out. The young plants give off a distinct odour of skunk. The smell gets weaker as they mature, but you can still get a whiff of it if you get close."

Doc squatted down to sniff the broad leaves of a thigh-high plant. "I see what you mean. Amazing. So, does anything eat them?"

"I'm told that bears and deer do, but you couldn't prove it by me. And I vaguely recall reading somewhere that some part of the plant is edible."

Now at the time, Doc was a medical officer involved with aerospace medicine at RCAF Station Trenton, Ontario. A Second World War veteran, he had interrupted his medical training to serve with the famous Pathfinders Squadron as a navigator, then returned to medicine when the war ended. He later attended a para-rescue course, which involved learning how to parachute into mountainous areas and dense forests, along with extensive wilderness survival skills. The topic still interested him.

"Which part do you figure is edible?" he asked.

"Beats me. But with the leaves smelling the way they do, I'd hazard a guess at the root."

Doc searched out a small plant and wrenched it from the ground, exposing a foot-long root that resembled a parsnip in shape and colour. He used his belt knife to sever the root, then partially peeled it, revealing firm white flesh. Paring off a slice about the diameter of a quarter, he popped it into his mouth. "Bitter as hell," he declared after a few seconds of vigorous chewing. "Very astringent ... it's making me salivate."

"Salivate" was an understatement. Doc suddenly started foaming at the mouth like a mad dog. I stared in wide-eyed horror as my seemingly hydrophobic companion stolidly continued chewing.

"Ma tong ish goin' numb," he calmly announced through a spray of white froth, "an' ma lipsh 'r tinglin'."

"Christ!" I croaked. "I hope you're not swallowing."

"Of corsh nod," he slurred, a Niagara of saliva pouring over his lower lip. "I'm nod crayshee."

He finally spat out the well-chewed piece of root and dabbed at his mouth with a handkerchief. "Wery inereshin'," he mumbled thickly, "bud I don' dink itsh da root dash edible."

The foaming ceased almost immediately and Doc's speech returned to normal in a minute or so, but it was at least 10 minutes before the numbness subsided from his lips and tongue.

That evening we searched my modest library of outdoor books to learn what we could about the swamp-loving plant. Despite Doc's reaction, we discovered that the entire plant is actually edible — but only after a lengthy cooking process.

According to ancient coastal Indian practices, the young leaves, stems, corncob-shaped spadices and roots are all simmered in several changes of water, which removes the musky smell and renders them edible. The root is then roasted and ground into flour, after which it requires a few weeks of aging before it is consumed. The writer claimed that bannock made from the flour is quite tasty.

Maybe it is, but the memory of Doc's effervescent flood of saliva effectively quelled any desire I might ever have to sample skunk cabbage, no matter how it's prepared.

THE LANGUAGE OF FISHING

Non-fishing friends — usually misguided souls who fritter away their lives indulging in questionable pastimes like golf or bowling — often ask me variations of the question, "Are all fishermen liars, or are all liars fishermen?" This from people who have graduated magna cum laude from the Baron Munchausen School of Creative Mathematics when it comes to keeping track of strokes or totalling scores.

True, when anglers get together, we do occasionally embellish some details a bit, but this is not a distortion of the truth so much as a means of spicing up a story to make it more interesting and entertaining. A very important point to bear in mind is that anglers seldom bother to record accurate details about any fish they have caught. We fish to enjoy ourselves, not to be slaves to bookkeeping. This was impressed upon me while I was still a fuzzy-cheeked youth prowling the banks of the Shuswap River for rainbows and bull trout. A grizzled old fly-fisherman, who suffered my presence only under duress, once advised me, "Don't ever weigh yer fish or measure 'em — jest 'guesstimate' 'em. That way you can make 'em as heavy or as long as you want without havin' to lie about it." Wise man, Old Will.

During 50-some years of fishing, I have met some master anglers who have elevated "guesstimating" to a fine art. It takes skill, practice and dedication, but can be a real boon now that catch-and-release is mandatory on many streams and trophy lakes. In fact, based on what some anglers have related to me, provincial fisheries managers should be elated to learn that the regulations are obviously working better than expected, because fish in these waters are far more numerous and much larger than they ever were when anglers could retain them for all to see.

Just as organized sports have outstanding professionals and the Olympics its gold, silver and bronze medalists, recreational angling has levels of superiority which many of us can only dream of ever attaining. Some anglers become so proficient at guesstimating they can determine the weight of lost fish, even ones which are never seen before their escape. These are usually monsters, and some have actually broken existing world records. A few, in fact, were so large and so absolutely unyielding in their strength and determination to stay deep, many of the anglers involved admitted that had they not been so cognizant and experienced, they might well have sworn they were snagged on bottom or in the kelp.

I should also point out that in virtually all cases where potential world record fish were lost, it was the result of unforeseen material or equipment failure — never, ever through any fault or miscalculation on the angler's part. As they will maintain, their skill and finesse at handling a rod and reel under the most adverse of conditions is the envy of all who hope someday to emulate them, and I have yet to meet one who has ever had a knot fail.

Most esteemed are those peerless paragons of truth who develop the uncanny ability to actually clone their catches. Admittedly, some only manage to double a single fish or two, but those with more experience become so skilled they can take a day totally devoid of anything remotely resembling a bite, and convert it into an outing filled with fish, all larger than average; each taken on a No. 24 Parachute Adams dry fly tied on the spot to match the hatch; and all caught and released while the story teller was fishing alone, out of sight around the river's bend, or, perhaps, hidden by an island on the lake or ocean. This is unfortunate, because these fish are always of trophy proportions except for the lone, barely legal-sized one kept because it was so badly hooked.

* * * *

I believe it is obvious from these few examples that the veracity of anglers is not in question; it is simply the inability of non-anglers to understand the technical terms and nuances of speech used by dedicated brothers and sisters of the rod and reel. It is unfortunate that, because others cannot comprehend our language, they resort to slurs and innuendo about our honesty. It would be easy to reply in kind by calling into question the thought process, or possible lack thereof, of people who hit, drop, roll or otherwise abuse totally inedible balls of varying sizes, weights and densities, but I think it is far better to pour oil on these troubled waters of confusion and avarice, in hopes of calming matters through education.

It is not my intent to try weaning non-fishing folks away from their preferred, albeit somewhat suspicious, forms of recreation, although once they realize we are not slaves to bookkeeping and number-crunching, our ranks could swell dramatically. However, I do believe it is only fair to clarify some common forms of communication anglers use among themselves, and in some cases, with spouses or significant others.

In addition to the size and quantity of fish, we discuss related activities that have nothing to do with guesstimating. In some cases, you might encounter a descriptive nuance known as a "slight understatement." An example would be an angler telling his wife, "I'm popping down to Gruntle's Tackle Emporium to pick up a few things." What he really means is, "I'm buying a new tackle box the size of a Dodge cube van and loading it up with bare necessities."

"You shouldn't need waders," actually means, "The river dries up this time of year."

I must caution that you should never jump to conclusions. If you mention a forthcoming summertime trip to the Quintessential River and your fishing buddy replies, "When I spent a week on the Quint' last year, we didn't have to use our sunscreen once," you might assume he means, "It rained the whole, damned time." However, you would be wrong. The actual translation is, "The clouds of mosquitoes were so thick that the sunlight couldn't penetrate them." You must be vigilant about watching for these variances of meaning in order to avoid confusion, but this is all part of the learning process. Experience will teach you that had there been torrential rains throughout his entire trip, he would have said, "You might find the river's a tad high that time of year, but there won't be any mosquitoes."

I have chosen a few other examples at random, with the actual meaning of each statement enclosed in brackets.

"Lake Noname? Didn't you hear that it winterkilled? A guy from the fisheries branch told me that a bad avalanche took the road out last winter, so they don't plan to restock it." (The road's a bit rough in spots, and it's absolutely crawling with big trout!)

"Bluegrouse Lake? It's been a write-off for two years now. A friend of mine tried it a couple of weeks ago and only got two little trout — and they were so muddy-tasting he couldn't eat them." (There are so many big, trophy-sized fish you'll be doing them a favour by keeping a few.)

"Woowoo Lake? It has some real problems — there are still lots of fish, but they're all stunted and absolutely riddled with worms." (You dog! How did you find out about my secret lake?)

In the "unforeseen circumstances" category are statements like, "The store at Extremely Remote Lake sells everything you need: food, cold beer, tackle, fishing licenses, gasoline...." (It changed hands and now deals exclusively in organic health food, natural-fibre clothing, and anti-fishing and hunting literature.)

"There are plenty of hotels and motels in town, so don't worry about reservations." (The Shriners Convention will be there at the same time as your planned vacation.)

Then there are "unfinished statements" like, "There won't be any mosquitoes this time of the year." (The blackflies kill them off.)

"There aren't any grizzlies or black bears in that entire area." (They're afraid of the rattlesnakes.)

"The road up is a bit steep in spots, but you won't have any problem." (As long as your four-wheel drive vehicle has a good winch.)

"You won't need chains." (If you happen to be driving a vehicle with Caterpillar tracks.)

"There was a slide near the top of Bottomless Gulch, so the road's a bit narrow, but you can make it through okay." (If you are riding a mountain bike.)

"From where you park, it's only a half mile to the lake." (Up a vertical mountain face that was recently clearcut and burnt over.)

Now, see if you have a handle on understanding the language of fishing by determining the true meaning of the following statements: "That salmon run shows up on the same day every year, just like clockwork."

"No sense in going too early, no one ever fishes there."

"They always have plenty of boats to rent."

"You won't need a bailing can."

"Don't bother with rain gear — it's always sunny during July and August."

Finally, a passing grade if you can determine the true meaning of this most commonly-heard statement: "I know a shortcut...."

EUPHEMISTICALLY SPEAKING

One of my favourite cartoons (circa early 1960s) depicts two uniformed members of the SPCA staring with shocked horror at the feet of a pedestrian jutting from beneath their truck. The driver is saying, "Oh dear! I think we've put him to sleep!" Which leads to my question: Why do so many people rely on euphemisms while using those nasty four-letter k... or d... words?

Hunters seldom speak of "killing" an animal or fowl; they "down," "bag," "drop" or "harvest" it. Game biologists "cull" and "control" herds, and pet owners have old, ill or unwanted animals put "under," "down" or "to sleep." Anglers usually "get" or "keep" fish — "Yep, we got five coho," or "Good day — three keepers." Those who fish for Atlantic salmon and steelhead are more honest when it comes to telling it like it is. They speak, for example, of four fish "beached" or "landed," of which three were "released" and one "killed."

Several years ago, I was hired to conduct fish-filleting demonstrations at the Toronto Sportsmen's Show. Since I had learned on West Coast, armour-plated rockfish, I found filleting walleye fairly simple. While I seriously doubted that anyone would be interested in watching someone fillet a fish, up to 200 people crowded around during some demonstrations, and several came back two or three times.

Toward the end of each session, I suggested that anyone with questions or advice, or who simply wanted to chat, could do so while I cleaned up my cutting board and knife. After one presentation, a young woman, probably in her mid-twenties, asked, "How do you ... ah ... put fish out of their misery?"

"Kill them?" I replied. She flinched slightly and nodded. I reached into the ice-filled cooler and selected a 1½-pounder. Laying it belly-down on the table, I placed my index fingertip on top of its head, slightly behind the eyes. "Hit them on the head with a club — right here," I said. "Hard! That way you only have to hit them once."

The woman looked as if she had just swallowed something bad tasting. "Not too hard," I continued, "otherwise, the eyes will pop out of their sockets. They'll definitely be dead, but they won't make for good photographs."

"That's disgusting!" she blurted, her eyes blazing and face flushed red.

"Madam," I said quietly, "you asked me how to kill a fish. It might seem disgusting to you, but it's the quickest, most humane way I know of — and I've killed lots of fish over the years."

She wheeled and stalked off in a proper snit, which several bystanders who had waited around seemed to find quite amusing. One elderly, white-haired woman slowly shook her head, then snorted and said, "I'll bet she never chopped off a chicken's head!"

"Your problem," remarked a bespectacled, scholarly young man, "is you said 'kill' instead of 'put to sleep'." He turned to the woman. "And I believe you should have said 'She has never surgically removed a chicken's respiratory and optical control centre'."

The young man had a point. It seems the only times those forbidden words are freely used is while we are discussing the anni-hilation of our own species. Switching on a radio or television set inundates us with the latest roster of violent deaths, often with far more graphic details than we really need or want to know. However, let a topic of conversation turn to creatures with fur, feathers or fins, and we revert to dragging out every tired, overused euphemism in the book. Hey! That's not a spade! That's a lightweight, portable, self-propelled, earth-moving device....

PUNCTURED

During the first year I knew Doc Hampson, he was promoted from wing commander to group captain and posted to RCAF Station

Winnipeg as the station medical officer. Since he was that much closer to Vancouver Island, we started planning more frequent get-togethers. When he arrived in early October to join me for some river coho fishing, Doc's botanical knowledge was expanded again by an encounter with another unusual plant that grows near most coastal streams.

The Tsolum, a small river north of Courtenay, often yielded some nice salmon, so we hiked a quarter mile into a fairly dependable stretch. Things proved slow at the first run, so I left Doc and walked upstream to a long pool, where I spotted several coho near the lower end. I headed back to get Doc, and found him already up on the trail.

He was holding his left hand up in a narrow shaft of bright sunlight that tunnelled through the forest canopy. Half-frame glasses perched on the end of his nose, head tilted well back, he was squinting closely at the back of his hand, turning it slowly from side to side, occasionally plucking at something with his right hand. Walking closer, I saw the stalks of several tall, spindly shrubs growing between the river and trail, and knew without asking what had happened.

"What's up?" I asked.

"What in hell are those … things?" Doc blustered, nodding toward the tan-coloured stalks.

"Devil's club."

He lowered his head and peered at me over the top of his glasses. "What a bloody good name. Is it local jargon or their proper name?"

"Proper."

"Very appropriate," Doc said drily. "And what sort of after-effects can I expect from all of these puncture wounds? Will assorted appendages start rotting and fall off?"

When I finally stopped laughing I replied, "Doubtful. They're a bit like wood slivers: if you pick 'em out, it heals pretty fast. If you miss any, they'll pus up and work themselves out — usually within a couple or three days. Sometimes longer."

Doc explained that his painful introduction to the bane of forest travellers occurred while he was climbing up the steep bank toward the trail. When he stubbed his toe against the ground-hugging lower stem of a shoulder-high plant, the jarring effect telegraphed up its slender, upright stalk, causing it to flail back and forth like a striking snake. It hit his hand only once, but over a dozen straw-coloured spines were embedded in his hide.

As prophesied, the injured area became mildly infected, and when Doc boarded the aircraft for Winnipeg two days later, he was still picking out stray spines as they worked to the surface.

* * * *

My first run-in with devil's club occurred when I was skinny-dipping in the Salmon River with Norman Dewflower, Curly Wallace and Dicky Bird. When we discovered that a recent cave-in on one of the river banks had revealed a mother lode of soft blue clay, it didn't take long before a spirited clay-ball fight erupted. Something like a snowball fight, except the clay didn't disintegrate when it smacked painfully into bare skin; it simply mushroomed and stuck. While attempting to evade one of these incoming missiles, I squatted and back-pedalled right into a clump of spine-covered stalks. But not for long. I have since had dozens of encounters with devil's club, all disagreeable, but none ever as painful or embarrassing.

Not all of my problems with devil's club involved punctures. Mother, an old-fashioned farm wife, considered it her bounden duty to concoct home remedies from whatever poked through the ground's surface. Feeling that anything as nasty as devil's club must have some saving grace, she mixed up a salve based on ground roots, the other main ingredients being lard and sulphur. Yellow, gritty, stinking sulphur that seared the lungs with its stench. I still cringe at the memory. Strained muscles or the faintest sign of a rash resulted in a thick, glutinous layer of the salve being slathered on the affected area to perform its mystical healing power.

This loving mother and wife, so normal in other ways, also brewed an herbal tea from the ground root of devil's club. Father and I were expected to put this foul-tasting concoction in our mouths and swallow it. Often several times before it finally stayed down. Never mind that neither of these medicaments ever did any detectable good, Mother would not be denied her self-appointed role as rural pharmacologist.

* * * *

Doc returned later that winter to chase steelhead. On our first day we got lucky, landing four fish each. Doc kept two dandies of 12 and 13 pounds. Our return trip to my car involved climbing the steep river bank. Weighted down with 25 pounds of steelhead in the rear pouch of his fishing vest, and carrying his rod in his left hand, Doc unconsciously reached out with his right hand and grabbed a sapling to help pull himself up. Only it wasn't a sapling. He let go immediately, but it was too late. Instantaneously, Doc had another collection of devil's club spines to keep him occupied for a few days, and I learned some new terminology that didn't exactly sound like it was medical in origin.

WORLD RECORDS

Back in 1992, writer Ron Nelson phoned from his home on the Queen Charlotte Islands to discuss the then-recent news of Art Lawton's 69 pound 15 ounce muskie being disqualified as a world record after 35 years. Our talk eventually turned to steelhead, of which we are both enamoured, and I mentioned that my largest ever landed was during the mid-1960s: an Oyster River buck measuring 44 inches. "I'm fairly sure of that," I explained, "because I used my rod to measure from the fork of its tail to its nose — twice. I was careful, too, because it was the biggest damned steelhead I'd ever seen, before or since. It measured from the rod's butt cap to the centre of the front binding on the second guide."

"Any idea how heavy it would have been?" Ron asked.

"I checked with guys who used to steelhead a lot on 'big fish' rivers like the Gold and Salmon, the Skeena and so forth — they guesstimated between 27 and 30 pounds. Other than size, what I remember most was the absolutely lousy fight — about two minutes and I had it beached in shallow water."

"What kind of shape was it in?"

"Fresh! Mint bright with a red blush on the cheeks and lateral line. A really fine-looking fish, Ron — deep, like a chinook, but it came in like a puppy dog."

"Well, I've got you beat by an inch," he said. No smugness, simply a statement of fact. "Forty-five inches. Mind you, I didn't have a ruler either, so I spanned it with my hand. And mine didn't fight very well, either. But all that aside, isn't it amazing, the lengths people will go to in order to get their names in the record books?"

"Yeah. And in most cases it's just that — their name in a book. But I figure the next person to catch a world-record largemouth bass or walleye will end up a millionaire. They're still the two most popular fish in North America."

Ron chuckled. "That's true. On the other hand, I doubt if the tackle or boat companies would beat a path to the door of someone who catches a new world-record carp or burbot."

"Ain't that the truth? There are even records for several species of suckers and sunfish — and eels."

"Have you noticed some people have their names in the record books a dozen times or more?" Ron asked.

"Yeah. Check out the salmon categories — one guy is listed over 40 times!"

"Definitely persistent. Have you ever considered trying for any of those line class records, Bob?"

"Once, a few years ago. Bryon Armstrong and I planned a trip to Goose Bay Resort, up in Rivers Inlet, to try for some all-tackle and line class records on the various rockfish that qualify: yelloweye, black, and vermilion — and maybe lingcod and halibut. We figured there were some attainable records, so I put together an outfit I thought would work well: a really soft-action, 13-foot noodle rod, and an old direct drive, free-spool Ambassadeur 1750 casting reel filled with six-pound test."

"And?..."

"Well, we went with good intentions and all of the necessary tackle, paperwork, cameras and whatnot, but there was a great run of coho going through, so we never even got around to rigging the long rod, let alone trying it out. Have you ever tried?"

"No. All that documentation and red tape doesn't really turn me on."

Later, after Ron decided he had donated enough money to the coffers of BC Telephone, I thought about the late Mr. Lawton and decided he will fade into well-earned obscurity since his supposed world-record muskie was proved a fraud. Just like Jurg Notzli, the Swiss angler who claimed a new world-record pike of 62 pounds 8 ounces in the early 1980s. Notzli enjoyed a brief fling at fame and fortune until it was discovered his trophy had been purchased from a commercial fisherman, who had netted the monster. Notzli was disqualified and received some free lodging at the Swiss government's expense to reflect upon what went wrong with his plan.

I thought also about my big Oyster River steelhead, wondering how close it might have come to a record. Digging out a recent copy of the National Fresh Water Fishing Hall of Fame record book, I discovered that the 12-pound test line class record steelhead was 23 pounds 6 ounces. Thus, if either extreme of those guesstimated weights made by my friends was close, my Oyster River fish would definitely have qualified.

Over the years, I have encountered a few other possible contenders, like the American angler who weighed in a 26-pound yelloweye rockfish at Port Hardy's Quarterdeck Marina, then gave it away for a barbecue. At the time, the world record was 21 pounds 4 ounces. Later that afternoon, Norma Cronmiller hauled a 24-pound yelloweye over the rail of Captain Ian Andersen's *Silver Fox* charter boat. It was delicious.

I have since caught three yelloweyes that would have broken that existing record by a pound or better, and have seen nearly a dozen others that were even larger than mine. Vera, my wife, caught one in 1992 that was easily 25 pounds, but we had no scales on board to verify it. We could have iced it down for a weigh-in at Port Hardy the following day, but were neither interested nor prepared to pursue any records, so it was photographed, then filleted and iced down.

Two days later, Vera and I joined Roger Clinton, then owner of the Port Hardy Pioneer Inn, for a run from nearby Coal Harbour to the mouth of Quatsino Sound, on the west coast of Vancouver Island. There, jigging in the lee of the Gillam Islands to avoid the surf, Roger caught his first ever vermilion rockfish. At 12 pounds and a bit, it was about three pounds over the record. Roger later reported that it made excellent fish and chips.

There was also the 24-pound bocaccio rockfish I pulled aboard the *Silver Fox* in 1988. My IGFA record book showed the all-tackle record as 21 pounds 4 ounces. We intended to eat that one, too, but the meat was so wormy I gave up in utter revulsion while filleting it, and have since faithfully released all bocaccio except occasional small ones that I keep for bait.

Back in 1950, I was a downy-cheeked 15-year-old working in a sawmill at Sugar Lake, in the North Okanagan. As there were no females of even a remotely similar age within reasonable hiking distance, my spare time was very sensibly devoted to fishing. One day, while fly-fishing for rainbows in the Shuswap River, I landed a 7 ¼-pound "Dolly Varden" on a 7X tippet rated at one-pound test. Since then, Interior Dollies have been biologically reclassified as "bull trout," but as either a Dolly or bull trout, my fish would have qualified as a two-pound test line class record.

During the early 1970s, while I was stationed with the air force in Ottawa, a friend steered me onto a tiny lake near Lakeview, Quebec, which supposedly held larger than average-sized smallmouth bass. He said I wouldn't catch many bass, but what I did catch would be big. As it turned out, other than a few fingerling bass and stunted yellow perch, I caught only one smallmouth that day, and it was truly big. However, like my trophy steelhead, its fight was virtually non-existent. From the time it grabbed my bucktail-skirted leadhead jig in 15 feet of water until I gripped it by the lower jaw and lifted it into the canoe, scarcely 20 seconds had elapsed.

My companion, Andy Sylvain, held his tape measure against the bass — 24 inches from tail fork to snout. We guesstimated its weight at better than eight pounds, then I eased it back into the tepid water. After a few moments, the largest live smallmouth bass either of us had ever seen, swam slowly and ponderously from view.

At a very conservative eight pounds, even 20 years later it would have been heavier than the Fishing Hall's 10-pound line class record of seven pounds seven ounces, and might even have given IGFA's 12-pound line class record of eight pounds eight ounces a run for its money.

None of my large fish, or those of my friends, were caught with any intention of establishing records. None would have qualified, anyway — not without proper documentation, written statements by witnesses, weigh-ins on certified scales, photographs and notarization. All a bit too officious and bureaucratic for folks who much prefer the flexibility of guesstimating the size of fish, which allows for adjustments to meet future requirements during mutual bragging sessions.

In the meantime, unless the IGFA and National Fresh Water Fishing Hall of Fame will accept my fishing rod measurements or Ron Nelson's hand spans as gospel, I fear the only place our names will ever appear in either publication is on their address labels.

REVENGE OF THE DOGFISH

A popularity poll would probably place dogfish at about the same level as blow flies and open cesspools. Maybe lower. Spiny dogfish, *Squalus acanthias*, can be encountered in the cool, temperate ocean waters of North America, Europe and Asia. Depending on their location they may go by the name of spur dog, thornback, grayfish, skittle-dog, bone-dog or cod shark.

Dogfish lack an anal fin, but make up for this oversight by having two dorsal fins, and in front of each is a sharply pointed spine that is mildly toxic. Punctures or cuts from these needle-like spurs affect people in different ways: some suffer no noticeable discomfort and heal almost overnight, while the wounds of others (my group) become inflamed and infected, and might take from days to weeks to clear up.

Those who have never handled dogfish might wonder how anyone could be clumsy enough to impale themselves on one of those spines. Believe me, it's easy. Dogfish can easily arch their tail higher than their head while hanging from a hook, and are almost eel-like in their attempts to tie their bodies in knots.

After you see the impressive array of dental structures possessed by huge sharks like great whites, makos and hammerheads, the rows of tiny nubbins lining the mouths of dogfish appear rather insignificant. Until you see what those little teeth do to the surface of a metal spoon, a hard plastic plug, or, heaven forbid, one of soft wood.

Close examination of a dogfish tooth shows that it looks much like a saw tooth. Each angles toward the outside of the jaw, greatly increasing its tearing ability. That the sharks' rasp-like rows of teeth are efficient is demonstrated when they attack hooked rockfish, which have hard scales and tough skin. The dogfish looks exactly like a miniature version of "Jaws" as it rolls on its side to swim close and grip its victim, then begins the typical shark-like tactic of twisting and writhing in order to jerk loose pieces of flesh.

Those who fish saltwater eventually encounter dogfish — often more of the pesky critters than ever thought possible. They are schooling fish, often massing in the tens of thousands. Which was the situation the first time I took Doc Hampson saltwater fishing.

After slowing our boat to trolling speed, I sliced the head from a frozen herring, rigged the "cut plug" to Doc's outfit, then lowered it over the side to check its performance. Satisfied that the bait was spinning properly, I handed him the rod. "Let out about 60 feet for starters," I suggested.

I had no sooner selected another frozen herring when Doc said, "I've got one already."

Even as I swung the boat's bow and slipped the outboard into neutral, I knew it wasn't a hoped-for coho. "You've got a dogfish."

"Have I really? Are they good to eat?"

"Supposedly — but I've never been that hungry."

"It looks just like a shark!" he exclaimed as the fish wallowed by our boat.

"That's because it is a shark," I said, reaching for his leader with my left hand. "Not very big, but a shark, nevertheless." In my right hand was my long-bladed filleting knife, its sharp edge up. Using the leader like a leash I guided the dogfish into position, then drove the knife point through its body from side to side, just behind the head. A quick pull up and back severed its spinal column and partially decapitated the fish. As blood billowed in the water, I reached down and finished severing the head. The entire operation took only two or three seconds.

"Now why did you do that?" Doc asked.

"Because hitting them on the head doesn't do anything, except make them harder to handle. This way, all I have to worry about is the head." I held the head by the snout, then used needle-nose pliers to wrench the trailing hook loose.

"Let's have a look at the head," Doc said.

Still holding it over the gunwale, I handed him the head. "Be careful of the teeth — it can still bite."

I had just started preparing another bait when Doc said, "I'll be damned — it bit me!" I glanced up and saw him holding his right hand at eye level, with the dogfish head suspended from the end of his thumb. "Oww! The damned thing's actually chewing on my thumb! Isn't that amazing? Oww!"

It required major surgery at the hinge of the dogfish's jaw with the point of my filleting knife to rid Doc of the head. The skin on the ball of his thumb was crisscrossed with shallow, slightly bleeding cuts, and his thumbnail was deeply scratched and scarred. While wrapping a Band-Aid around the wound I asked, "Why, pray tell, did you stick your thumb in its mouth?"

"I wanted to feel how sharp its teeth are."

"Well?"

Doc looked at me for a moment, then shrugged. "Now I know."

DIFFERENT STROKES

No matter where or how anglers choose to fish, there are usually well-known flies, lures or baits to use, and specific tactics that work better than others. However, there are never any absolutes. A few anecdotes to illustrate....

General Sir Charles Loewen once told me about fishing for Atlantic salmon in Northern Ireland during the 1930s. One weekend he decided to fish a river bordering the artillery garrison he commanded. When he arrived at the river, his "batman" (officer's servant) was there, fishing a deep pool. Noticing a cork bobber on the water, the general asked the gunner what he was fishing for.

Loewen chuckled as he recalled, "He said he was fishing for salmon. I asked what he was using on his line, and he said a worm. It was obvious the poor fellow knew nothing about fishing for salmon, so I went into a lengthy discourse about how salmon didn't feed when they returned to the rivers, and could only be taken with lures or flies. He reeled in while I was talking, and when I finally finished he thanked me for my information, then bade me good afternoon, walked over to a nearby tree and picked up two beautiful salmon of about 15 and 20 pounds."

During the early 1950s, while I was fly-fishing the Shuswap River below Sugar Lake, a middle-aged angler paused to ask me how the fishing was. As we chatted, I studied his tackle: a six-foot-long, split-cane trolling rod that had seen better days, and a hefty Penn multiplier filled with braided line that looked suitable for towing trucks. A gang troll about three feet long dangled from his rod tip, its nickel-plated willow leaf blades clanging musically like wind chimes. After we finished talking, he walked well upstream and waded out to a granite outcropping in midstream. Drawing a Prince Albert pipe-tobacco can from his shirt pocket, he took out a worm to bait his snelled hook.

He pulled about 50 feet of line from his reel and coiled it carefully on the rock shelf, then made a strip-cast to swing the gang troll about 15 feet out into the current. As the spinner blades caught in the edge of the fast water, he held his rod tip high while paying out the remaining line. When it reached the end, his sturdy rod bowed momentarily, then eased off somewhat as the troll swung into a slow-running backwater. He had just started reeling in when a foot-long rainbow trout struck his hook.

Over the next hour or so, he repeated his slow, almost agonizing procedure of stripping line from the reel, carefully coiling it so it wouldn't tangle, casting, then retrieving. He missed and lost a few fish, but in less than an hour his efforts yielded four more similar-sized trout. Not a great catch for that river in those days, but not bad considering his tackle. After getting to know him better, I learned it was all he owned at the time.

Frank Gavin and I once decided to try for summer steelhead in the Heber River. After we skidded down a steep bank leading to the Iron Gate Pool, Frank sat down and lit a cigarette while I worked over the deep pool with my fly rod. About 30 steelhead were loosely schooled in the crystal water near the pool's head, but my offerings were ignored. Totally. A few fish even moved aside to avoid my sunken fly if it drifted too close. After 20 minutes of being snubbed, I stepped back and said, "See what you can do."

Frank started with a tiny No. 0 gold Mepps. Nothing. He worked up through a No. 1 and 2, then tried the same sizes in silver. Zip. While rummaging through his tackle bag, he suddenly grinned and said, "Well, if they won't co-operate, I'll scare 'em to death." He held up a three-inch-long Super Duper, an odd-looking spoon shaped like a narrow, elongated U, with the hook fastened at the bend. Frank said it had been a good lure for Ontario bass, so he had decided to recycle it. It was originally black but he had given it an undercoat of white paint, followed by bright fluorescent orange. It looked absolutely ridiculous.

"I'd better check its action," Frank said, casting toward the pool's tail. His heavy lure smacked down loudly on the surface, then plummeted toward bottom before he had even started to retrieve. At this point every steelhead in the pool turned and raced toward that gaudy-looking apparition like a school of ravenous piranha. One of the smaller fish was first to reach the lure, and promptly hooked itself.

Shortly after the five-pounder was beached, the milling steelhead calmed down and returned to the pool's head. Thinking they might now be in a more favourable mood, I tried my flies once again, but to no avail. I gave up, whereupon Frank moved back into position and once more cast to the pool's tail. Again the steelhead swarmed his lure, but during the melee Frank let it sink too deep and snagged bottom. Permanently. And we never hooked another fish that day.

On one of the chilly, dismal days that were all too common during July, 1993, Ralph Shaw and I set out in his 17-foot Boston Whaler to jig for salmon off the southern ends of Denman and Hornby islands. For two hours we drew a complete blank, putting our enthusiasm on par with the weather. Then, while we were drifting across the mouth of Tribune Bay, the clouds started breaking up and the day, if not the fishing, seemed to improve a bit.

More out of boredom than anything remotely resembling strategy, I lobbed my 1½-ounce perch Zzinger about 200 feet from the boat. I started reeling as fast as my Ambassadeur 6000C permitted, and promptly hooked a coho. After netting the seven-pounder, I fired another long cast in the same direction. A 15-pound chinook hit before my lure travelled 20 feet. That's a guesstimate as the fish came unstuck after a fast flurry of jumps, but a marginally under-sized chinook of seven or eight pounds quickly grabbed the lure as I continued retrieving it.

Two casts had produced more action than we'd seen all morning, so I gave it some thought: For no reason other than the boat's position, both casts had been directly toward the sun. Many trollers maintain they get more bites while moving away from the sun than toward or parallel to it. They theorize that fish don't like looking into bright sunlight any more than we do. Whatever the reason, I agree with the practice. Curious, I cast parallel to the sun. Nothing. Ditto for a cast the other way. My third cast directly at the sun yielded another borderline sublegal chinook, convincing me to keep squinting and casting in that direction.

During the next two hours I tangled with five more undersized chinooks, two much larger ones in the 20-pound range — both lost through great skill and cunning on my part — and a twin to my first coho. Ralph stayed with standard "controlled drop" and "lift-drop" jigging tactics throughout. Hah! He, who usually outfishes me at an absolutely embarrassing ratio, managed only two sublegal chinooks, thereby causing an almost terminal case of gloat on my part.

Several years ago, Big Bill Jesse and I were fishing Fry Lake, west of Campbell River. Well, the truth is we were getting lots of fresh air and casting practice, but no fish. While continuing our search along the shoreline, we spotted a fellow angler, a teen-ager who looked like he had just found a spinning outfit and was trying to figure out how it worked. Holding the rod upside down with the reel on top, he would pull line from the spool, then pinch it against the rod handle with his thumb as the bail was opened. Holding the rod handle with both hands, he would lower the tip almost to the ground behind him, then flail it forward over his shoulder, causing his large sinker and lure to rocket almost straight up for 40 feet, arc over, then splash down about 30 feet from shore.

"Do you see what he's usin' for a lure?" Bill whispered incredulously as we walked close enough to see him more clearly. I nodded. Suspended about a foot from a one-ounce Peetz sinker was a bright yellow-and-red, cork-bodied bass popper, a worm dangling from its feathered hook. "And do you see what's layin' on the ground behind him?" Bill continued, his whisper approaching a steam whistle in volume. Again I nodded. A deep-bodied cutthroat trout that looked to be all of 20 inches long, plus two of about 16 inches.

After striking up a conversation with the youth, we discovered he was indeed brand-new to fishing. No, he didn't know what kind of lure it was, but he had decided to use it because "it looks really neat." Both it and the sinker were tied on with what appeared to be assorted Molly Hogans and overhand knots.

Normally, Bill and I would have taken time to coach the lad and offer some friendly advice on all of the things he was doing wrong, but he seemed to be having too much fun. Besides, why tinker with success? We simply congratulated him on his fish, then wandered off, pondering Fate's warped sense of humour.

GUIDE FROM HELL

"Don't horse it!" my guide bellowed, eyes protruding beneath two large, throbbing veins in his forehead, his voice worthy of a regimental sergeant major. "You'll break it off!"

True, my 12-foot-long rod was bent into a fairly good imitation of an inverted letter L, but I had neglected to tell my guide I was field testing a "noodle rod," a very flexible rod design that became popular in Ontario and the Great Lakes states around the late 1970s. Then the early 1980s, the manufacturer had sent me a new model to evaluate for possible use by West Coast anglers. Which was precisely what I was doing.

I was less interested in landing the fish than in learning what sort of abuse the rod could take. I determined almost immediately that there was little danger of breaking it, for "noodle" was an apt description of its action, although the term should have been preceded by "wet." I was holding the handle almost straight up, but over half of the shaft was submerged. However, while it probably appeared to my distraught guide that I was unmercifully horsing the unseen chinook salmon charging around beneath our boat, the actual pressure being exerted was minimal.

"But I like horsing 'em," I said amiably, cocking the rod handle back until it rested more or less horizontally on my right shoulder. The shaft was now almost a complete circle. "Look," I continued. "I'll bet I can touch the rod tip with the butt cap." I leaned forward to do so.

"Argh! You're gonna lose it!" my guide shrieked, lurching halfway from his seat as though he might let go of the outboard tiller to snatch the rod away from me. At which point the straining shaft of graphite suddenly straightened.

"Past tense," I said. "I'm not 'gonna lose it'; I have lost it."

"You bleepedy-bleep ham-handed bleeping idiot!" he ranted, spittle spraying from his lips. "You broke the bleeping line!" Some guides take their jobs far too seriously, totally lacking anything which remotely resembles a sense of humour, while others suffer from personality disorders that range from profoundly melancholic to potentially homicidal. I was obviously saddled with a guide possessing all of the above.

I didn't bother responding to his nonstop ranting because I was puzzled about why the fish got off. Despite my feigned ham-handedness, I knew there had been nowhere near enough pressure to break that 15-pound-test leader.

I continued cranking the handle of my single-action reel. As the four-ounce keel sinker popped through the surface, the wind caught the 12-foot leader and it billowed into the air. I lifted the rod to swing the sinker in close enough to grab, then pulled in the trailing strand of monofilament and studied the free end. I leaned forward, holding it toward my guide and asked, "Would you mind giving me your so-called 'professional' opinion about what might have happened here?"

His eyes narrowed and he bit off a curse in mid mutter. Although I was using my own tackle, I'd had no leaders tied up beforehand, so had used one of his. The last inch looked like a miniature corkscrew, indicating the line hadn't broken after all; his knot had come untied.

I kindly offered to give my guide a few pointers on tying knots properly, but he leaped to his feet, bellowing, "Don't give me that crap! There's a bite on!"

We exchanged seats and Crony grabbed his rod. It was his turn to fish while I ran the outboard — and perfect my own version of being the "guide from hell."

JUST LIKE JASON LUCAS

My childhood in the Fraser Valley was followed by jobs in sawmills and logging camps in the North Okanagan and the Cariboo. Throughout these years my fishing involved mostly rainbow trout, bull trout and mountain whitefish. During a three-year stint in the army, I always took my annual leave from Fort Osborne Barracks, in Winnipeg, Manitoba, and returned to the Okanagan, where I fished the Shuswap River, Sugar and Echo lakes, or hiked into Rainbow Lake (now called Spectrum Lake). A few months of civilian life convinced me that I missed wearing brass buttons, so I re-enlisted in the air force in 1957. After training as a munition and weapons technician at Camp Borden, Ontario, I was posted to RCAF Station Comox, on the central eastern shore of Vancouver Island.

Once the dust had settled from moving into a new home, then getting familiarized with working at my new job in the Armament Section, I had time to check out the fishing prospects. They looked very good indeed. In addition to several nearby lakes which all held rainbow and cutthroat trout, there were steelhead and sea-run cutthroat, five species of Pacific salmon, and virtually dozens of salt-water bottom fish species. However, while I felt like I had died and gone to Angling Heaven, something always seemed to be missing. As a devout reader of American outdoor magazines since childhood, I had developed a desire to fish for largemouth and smallmouth bass, pike, muskie and walleye. This remained only a dream until the early

1960s, when I discovered that several southern Vancouver Island lakes held smallmouth bass, and one of them — Spider Lake — was only 30 miles from our home in Comox.

Charged with youthful enthusiasm and a tackle box filled with huge, mostly homemade plugs, spoons and spinners, I headed for Spider Lake. Dawn was breaking when I arrived, quivering with anticipation at thoughts of smallmouths dancing on the surface, just like the paintings that illustrated the marvellous stories in *Sports Afield* written by Jason Lucas, the freshwater fishing editor. As the midsummer sun climbed high in a cloudless sky, I stalked the irregular shoreline, flogging the water to a froth. Along deep stretches my lures snagged on submerged trees and broke off; along shallow, weedy stretches they snagged on submerged rocks and broke off. I got plenty of knot-tying practice, but not so much as a glimpse of any smallmouth bass. It was almost midnight when I arrived home — dog tired, sunburnt, mosquito-bitten and dispirited, with my tackle box near empty. Spider Lake's smallmouth bass were obviously a myth.

The following evening, I related my tale of woe to a fellow angler at the Lorne Hotel pub in Comox. Ernie laughed and said, "I know how you feel — that's what happened to me the first time I went to Spider Lake. But there are bass there, Jonesy — I've caught them."

"How?"

Ernie drained his glass, glanced at his watch and replied, "Gotta go."

"Wait!" I waved frantically at the waiter. "Let me buy you a beer."

"Well — if you insist." With a full glass before him, Ernie continued, "I went down with a whole bunch of the wrong lures, too. I found out later they were all too big — better suited for largemouth bass. It was hot as hell, and by lunch time I'd beaten my way about half way around the lake and lost most of my lures. I was absolutely bushed, so I found a shady spot on one of the points where I could sit and eat lunch. The bottom dropped off fairly fast and there wasn't too much crap in the water, so I tied on a silver spinner with a snelled hook and crimped on a sinker for weight. I had some worms, so I stuck a big one on the hook and tossed it out, propped my rod up on a rock, then sat in the shade to chow down."

Ernie paused and lubricated his throat with a healthy glug of beer. "About 10 minutes later the rod tip twitched like a little one was nibblin' — the first action I'd had all day. I jumped up and grabbed the rod, but then I calmed down and waited until the line started to tighten before I set the hook. It was a smallmouth, Jonesy — about three pounds."

"On a worm?"

He nodded. "Yep — dirty old garden hackle. And I caught three more before I headed home — all about two pounds or better."

"Did they fight?"

"Yeah! Real good, too. They don't run like a trout, but they're about as strong. They jump and charge around, and do a kind of hula dance on top of the water. It's really quite a sight."

Another beer divulged that Ernie's catch hadn't been a fluke. He had returned to Spider Lake on other occasions, and enjoyed reasonable success each time. He also discovered the advantage of wearing polarized sun glasses. "You can actually see them just hanging there about three or four feet under the surface. Don't cast too close or you'll spook 'em. Flip the worm out about 10 feet to one side of them, then let it sink to the bottom. About five times out of 10 they'll eventually go after it, but there's a better way...."

Through trial and error, Ernie had discovered that suspending a worm beneath a small bobber attracted bass better than those sunk right on the bottom. "Put the split shot on your line just under the bobber, enough so it barely floats. That way, the bass don't seem to notice it when they take the worm. They'll swim off a bit and the bobber'll go down — but don't do anything. The bobber'll come up after a few seconds — then go down again. If it stays down more than five seconds, start counting to 30 — real slow — then set the hook. But if it comes up, you have to start all over again. I've waited right up to a minute and never hooked one of 'em deep. Always in the lip ... always."

* * * *

I returned to Spider Lake a few days later with a supply of fresh worms, a couple of clear plastic torpedo floats, some split-shot sinkers, and a new pair of polarized sunglasses. Scarcely two minutes after starting to prowl the sloping shoreline, I spotted my first bass about 20 feet out. It was suspended about four feet below the surface, and almost facing me. Following Ernie's advice, I carefully lobbed the bobber and worm about 10 feet to the fish's left. Nothing happened for about 30 seconds, then it slowly cruised over to investigate the worm. Fascinated, I watched it advance right up to the worm, stop, then suddenly back away — the first time I had ever seen a fish swim backwards.

The bass advanced again, nipped the worm between its lips, then swam downward out of sight. As Ernie had prophesied, the bobber submerged for a few seconds, then slowly reappeared with the worm still hanging below. Eventually, up came the bass to once more grip the worm, then swim downward again. Several seconds passed, then the bobber resurfaced a few feet farther out. I waited. After going down the third time, it remained out of sight for the required five seconds, so I started counting. At 30 I reared back on the spinning rod and felt the solid weight of a fish.

The fight was unlike anything I had ever experienced with trout or salmon. Rather than long, reel-screeching runs and high, twisting leaps, the smallmouth stayed close, executing a couple of tail-over-head cartwheels that barely cleared the surface, then thrusting its body partly from the water to skitter across the surface in a shimmying tail-dance. It looked exactly like the paintings which illustrated those marvellous stories by Jason Lucas.

When it dove toward a sunken snag, burrowing down with surprising strength and determination, I jammed my fingertip against the spool and snubbed it up short. The six-pound test line hummed like a high-tension power line, threatening to snap from the strain. Amazingly, it held and the fish turned just short of reaching the branches. The tussle lasted a minute or two longer, then I led the bass in close enough to grasp its lower jaw between my thumb and curled forefinger — just like Jason Lucas did in the photographs. Admittedly, I did it cautiously, this being the first time I had ever tried it, but it worked.

That 2½-pounder marked the beginning of an enjoyable association with smallmouth bass that has continued ever since; interrupted for a few years by two postings to Germany, then accelerated again by two postings to Southern Ontario.

After returning to Vancouver Island in 1980, I found interest in smallmouth bass had increased, but the lakes containing them are seldom crowded. Understandable, perhaps, in the midst of trout and salmon country; however, much as I love fishing the rivers and salt-water, there is a lot to be said for occasionally taking time out for smallmouths. On cool summer or early autumn evenings, it is pleasant drifting in a boat on the mirrored surface of a small lake, probing the shoreline with a floating plug or a tiny bass bug of spun deer hair. Smallmouths seldom take such offerings gently; some leap into the air beside your lure and grab it on the way down, while others attack from below with such ferocity that the surface erupts with loud, startling explosiveness. Then, when smallmouth bass begin their cartwheeling, tail-walking dance across the surface, looking just like they did in *Sports Afield*, there is no doubt that they add a generous helping of spice to the life of this aging angler.

WHAT'S IN A NAME?

Although names are used for identification, there is always room for confusion. Like at the 1984 Outdoor Writers Association of America annual convention in Traverse City, Michigan. Homer Circle, the resident fishing guru at *Sports Afield* magazine, glanced at my name tag, smiled, then stuck out his hand. I assumed he remembered me from two previous conventions we had both attended. As he clasped my hand, the man affectionately known as "Uncle Homer" said, "Bob Jones! I want you to know I'm a real fan of your work."

Flabbergasted doesn't begin to describe my feeling. One of North America's most popular outdoor writers a fan of my work? "Thank you," I answered.

"I haven't had a chance to get downstairs to see the display," Uncle Homer continued. "Are you showing any paintings?"

"Paintings? I'm not a painter."

"Aren't you Bob Jones, the painter from Delaware?"

"No, I'm Bob Jones the writer — from Vancouver Island."

Uncle Homer's puzzlement turned to obvious disappointment.

"Oh, I'm sorry. Ahh ... what sort of stuff do you write?..."

So much for fame.

While my friends actually do call me Bob, my byline usually appears as Robert H. Jones because there are other writers in various fields named Bob Jones, and a few who go by Robert Jones, either with or without a centre initial. One used to be the men's fashion editor for a glossy, general interest magazine. This caused much mirth among those familiar with my wardrobe, which leans heavily toward denim, wool, neoprene and duct tape.

Mispronunciation also creates confusion. My friend Bruce Masterman is a staff reporter and outdoor columnist for the *Calgary Herald* newspaper. Bruce says he has grown used to people converting his last name to Masterson, but draws the line at devout members of the politically correct movement dubbing him Masterperson.

"Outdoor Writers of Canada" clearly identifies a national organization of professional writers. However, someone found it confusing enough that members attending a meeting at a Toronto hotel were greeted by a sign in the lobby welcoming the "Outdoor Riders of Canada." The hotel staff seemed genuinely relieved when we didn't arrive on horseback or motorcycles.

Some names are harder to pronounce than others, at least in the beginning. I have several friends in Japan, which has meant learning names like Takeshi, Tadyoshi, Etsuo, Noboru, Shinichi, Hiroyuki, Masanao, Toshikazu, Haruo, Nagaharu, Tochihiko, Utako and Fukuko. Difficult, but not as much as some of our more common names are for them. A few years ago, Vera and I hosted a Japanese friend at our home for several weeks. Hajime "Jim" Omori was a skilled fly-fisherman and tier, so I introduced him to as many of my fishing cronies as possible. Although Jim's knowledge and use of English was excellent, he was still experiencing difficulty with words beginning with "R." One evening, after returning from a Steelhead Society of B.C. meeting, he remarked wistfully, "Your friends are very nice, but they have such difficult names: Randy, Rory, Ralph, Richard, Robert, Rusty,..."

I laughed. "Don't worry, Jim. After a couple of weeks you'll be able to say 'Randy, Rory, Ralph, Richard, Robert and Rusty ride red rubber rafts through the raging rapids'."

"Not me!" he protested. "My poor tongue could never stand that much abuse."

While I was stationed at Baden-Soellingen, Germany, with the RCAF, friends there did the best they could with my name. The letter J is pronounced as Y in German, and the letter E is also said aloud. Thus, my last name came out Yown-ess, and my first name was Boob — but I'd rather forget that.

REINVENTING THE WHEEL

Although it often seems the fishing-tackle industry keeps busy reinventing the wheel, what appears to be the recycling of old ideas or concepts usually has more to do with incorporating advances in new materials than running out of fresh ideas. The introduction of space-age fibres like Kevlar, Spectra and Dyneema in the early 1990s is a good example. When I started fishing during the early 1940s, lines were made of twisted or braided linen. These were eventually replaced by braided nylon, and by the early 1950s monofilaments had become the line of choice for most anglers. The main hold-outs were big game fishing specialists, who continued using the basically no-stretch linen lines until braided Dacron appeared about the mid-1950s. Nylon and Dacron ruled the roost until early 1993, when lines braided from the new materials appeared and captured the attention of anglers.

Thanks to new generations of graphite fibres, plus some truly innovative changes to structural and ferrule designs, a few manufacturers offer multi-piece rods that handle and cast as well as one- and two-piece models. This is of particular appeal to anglers who travel a lot, especially by air, as some nine-foot-long fly rods break down into four 28-inch sections that fit easily into carry-on luggage.

Even fishhooks continued improving. "Ultra-sharp" models showed up in the late 1980s, winning over a large segment of the angling population. Hooks were traditionally plated with bronze, nickel, cadmium and gold, but manufacturers started offering models with silver, gray, black or red anodized finishes that cut down dramatically on corrosion.

Some interesting changes have occurred with soft plastic baits, the most noteworthy being what finally appears to be the successful incorporation of long-lasting, fairly permanent scents. It took a while before it all came together. Artificial worms fashioned from rubber were first patented in the 1860s, then 20 years later, William Mills & Son of New York introduced a line of rubber insects. Abercrombie & Fitch produced a rubber worm mounted on three tandem hooks during the early 1900s, but like its predecessors, it failed to catch on because the material was simply too stiff to be lifelike. The first breakthrough came in 1935, when the B.F. Goodrich Rubber Company marketed a genuinely soft, flexible vinyl plastic called Koroseal.

Although a few small manufacturers produced lures of moulded vinyl prior to the Second World War, they did not become popular until 1949, when Nick Creme of Tyler, Texas, introduced Creme Worms. These soft plastic lures forever changed North American largemouth bass fishing techniques, and as time passed, other fishing methods were also affected. Anglers quickly discovered that a short piece of plastic worm on a leadhead jig produced walleye, smallmouth bass, crappie and assorted panfish. West Coast steelheaders took longer to adapt, but when some suitable colours were eventually offered, a method to effectively rig and fish the worms evolved, and they became quite popular.

The use of scents for attracting fish is lost to antiquity, but might well have originated through the use of "chumming" — introducing ground-up bait into the water to attract fish. Then again, it might have been the first time a fisherman spit on his bait. Whatever the origins, various preparations have been around for years, the most common of which is oil of anise.

About 1960, I recall some West Coast steelheaders using a concoction consisting of walnut-sized pieces of sponge rubber, which were liberally smeared with a messy salmon-egg paste that smelled suspiciously like rancid cod liver oil. Fortunately, it wasn't too long before soft plastic "Gooey Bobs" hit the B.C. market. There was some initial hesitation in their acceptance, but those of us who tried the licorice-smelling lures were pleasantly surprised to discover they actually caught fish.

The modern line of scents appeared during the late 1970s, then started attracting serious attention in the early 1980s. There were certainly some notable advances, but also some better-forgotten duds. About 1978, while living in Ontario, I was given a slim, minnow-shaped plug to field test. It bore something of a resemblance to an original Rapala, but its porous plastic body was impregnated with some magic elixir that the enclosed advertising brochure claimed would "REVOLUTIONIZE FISHING!!" I cast and trolled that plug in stretches of the Rideau River I knew to be virtually crawling with fish, and finally caught a stunted little rock bass. Right in the anus. This was duly reported to the manufacturer, along with a suggestion that the fish might have been making a social comment about the worth of their lure. For some reason I have never determined, they never sent me anything else to field test.

Shortly after the newer generation of scents started appearing, I fell heir to several small plastic bottles filled with samples of liquid scents, which, the accompanying pamphlet claimed, would "REVOLUTIONIZE FISHING!!" Maybe the same advertising firm worked for both companies. I sorted through the bottles — catfish, muskie/pike, walleye, bass, rainbow, lake trout and — saltwater. Bingo! That sample was tossed into my tackle box for future reference. Later, while killing some time at a local wharf, I dangled a 1/32-oz. jig in the water, which soon attracted a school of shiners. Although they wouldn't bite, they swarmed around the lure in a large, squirming ball of curiosity. After adding a drop of scent to the jig, I again lowered it into the milling school. Every fish within a one-foot radius of the lure darted away and refused to come any closer. It was like looking down an empty glass tube, two feet in diameter, surrounded by shiners.

On another occasion, Ralph Shaw and I tested a semi-solid saltwater bait that could be moulded onto a hook. Most times it simply fell off within a few seconds, and the rare times it didn't, we caught nothing but dogfish. Which proved nothing because we do that a lot, anyway.

When well-known author and television personality Charlie White was making his series of excellent underwater films about salmon fishing, his findings revealed that if scented and unscented lures were trolled side-by-side, salmon almost always hit the scented one. Never mind that the foul-smelling, oily water from his boat's bilge seemed to be a most attractive scent; the point is that once a salmon started following the lures, scent definitely made a difference.

Salmon are schooling fish that swim actively over great distances in search of food, so sight probably plays the most important role in drawing their attention to a possible meal. Flashers and dodgers are often used as attractors to tempt salmon close enough to see a lure or bait, and while there is no guarantee they will then bite it, fresh or frozen herring or anchovy might have a distinct edge over lures because of their scent. Thus, it is reasonable to assume that if one is using lures rather than bait, the addition of a suitable scent will enhance its appeal. Not being an advertising writer I won't claim this will "REVOLUTIONIZE FISHING!!" when fish are slow to bite unbaited lures, but it certainly couldn't hurt.

§THREE
STEELHEAD SAGAS

THE BET

"Remember the time you waded across the Puntledge, just above the hatchery?" asked Big Bill Jesse. I waited, knowing he didn't really expect an answer. "That water was just sluicin' through — right up to your waist — and I was sure we'd be playing 'Taps' over your empty coffin at the base chapel. But you went across that river just like you knew what you were doing. Damn! — that was as classic a piece of wading as I've ever seen. Then you stepped up on top of that skinny little finger of gravel, tripped and fell right on your face on the other side, and like to have drowned your dumb ass off in six inches of water!"

Big Bill and I went back to when we still wore air force uniforms — he for the Yanks, me the Canucks. We met at RCAF Station Comox when he was posted there to USAF Detachment 5. Bill tracked me down at work and started badgering me to take him steelhead fishing. After initially putting him off, I finally relented and agreed to take the big master sergeant steelheading — but only once. As it turned out, it started a friendship that spanned 30 years.

After retiring from the USAF, Bill and Delores settled in Washington state. When I shed my own uniform, Vera and I returned to Vancouver Island, close enough to visit back and forth fairly frequently. However, after they moved to Florida in the mid-1980s, our visits dwindled to a few days once a year, when they drove north. In the beginning, Bill and I usually sneaked off for an afternoon or two of salmon fishing, but eventually we were just as happy sitting around yarning about past experiences. The only problem being, of course, there was a lot of selectiveness to our recollections.

When we finished chuckling over my tangle-footed wading, I said, "Remember the time at the Little Oyster Pool when I got the backlash that took me half an hour to pick out?"

"I certainly do," Bill replied, "but I'd rather forget it."

On my first cast I had brought my rod tip back too far, lowering my bait into the water behind me. When I cast, line exploded from my level-wind reel, forming a ball of loose monofilament the size of a grapefruit. I waded ashore to start picking, plucking and tugging.

Bill was quite sympathetic, chortling, "Why, I believe I have this entire pool to myself for most of the afternoon." Whereupon he started working it thoroughly from top to bottom, but to no avail. When I finally finished my chore and stood up, Bill said, "About time! C'mon, let's go."

"Not likely," I said, lobbing a quartering cast upstream. "I came to fish."

"Listen, I've covered every inch of this pool — there ain't no fish here."

"Just because you can't catch them doesn't mean they aren't here," I replied, throwing down the proverbial gauntlet.

"Is that right?" he blustered. "Well, I'll tell you what: if you catch a damned steelhead in here I'll buy you a beer at Fishermen's Lodge."

"A beer?" I repeated. "One lousy beer?"

"I'll buy you two. Hell, I'll buy you three beers if you catch a steelhead in here — but you buy me two if you don't. Well?"

"You're on," I said, lifting my rod tip to set the hook on the steelhead that had been mouthing my bait as we haggled. And despite Big Bill racing around the pool like a madman, knife in hand as he tried to slash my line, I even managed to land and release it.

SHIFTING ON THE FLY

Alf, a middle-aged friend with an enviable reputation as a steelhead fisherman, confided he wanted to take up fly-fishing for the sea-run rainbow trout. "What do you think?" he asked.

I countered with my own question: "Have you ever fly-fished before?"

"Nope. Don't know anything about it."

"So, why this sudden urge to switch?"

Alf thought for a moment, then answered, "Challenge. A few years ago I started getting bored with steelheading. The fun had gone out of it because it was too easy. Got so bad I almost gave it up, but then I decided to quit using bait and switch strictly to lures." He shook his head and chuckled, "Now that put things in a different light. I could still catch 'em, but not anywhere near as many. It wasn't as though I'd never used lures before — but I'd always had roe to fall back on.

"It got pretty frustrating at times, but I stuck it out because it was a real challenge. I'd know the fish were there, but there was more to it than drifting a gob of roe by their noses. I had to figure out what would turn them on — which lure, which colour, which presentation, which angle of approach. By the end of that first season I had a pretty good handle on things, and my catch success climbed right back up there. Now I'm starting to get bored again, and I see more and more guys fly-fishing, so...."

Alf was serious about switching, so I explained that the change would be much more dramatic and involved than simply eliminating bait in favour of artificial lures. "You'll have to learn an entirely new form of fishing: casting techniques, timing, line control, line densities, sink rates, leader tapers — plus a whole new set of terminology. Learning the basics of casting isn't anywhere near as difficult as some people might have you believe, Alf, but casting's only one part of the game.

"Fly-fishing won't produce anywhere near the numbers of steelhead, either, even after you learn the ropes. You'll run into lots of situations where you simply can't cover the water — places where you can't get close enough, or it's too overgrown to cast, or there's too much fast water between you and the fish — the type of jackpots you could handle fairly easily with your drift rod."

"So, are you trying to tell me I should forget about it?" he asked.

"No — I'm just pointing out the negative side so you don't go into it thinking you can master it in a week or two. Believe me, Alf, there are more positives than negatives, and once you get the hang of it, it's lots of fun."

"Yeah? Well, just out of curiosity, if it's so much fun, how come you don't fly-fish all the time?"

"Too restrictive for someone in my line of work, Alf. I write about all types of fishing, so if I stuck to only one method it would narrow my point of view. Like Crony would say, 'Viewing the big, wide world through a cocktail straw.' I try balancing it so I do a bit of everything."

At my suggestion, Alf asked the advice of a few more fly-fishers, and read whatever he could buy or borrow on the topic. He then acquired a basic outfit and set about learning the fundamentals of casting, timing, rhythm and rod manipulation. He practised on his back lawn until he was satisfied with his performance, then moved on to one of the rivers — and quickly learned about things like over-hanging branches, steep banks that foiled his attempts to cast, hooks that broke on rocks when a back cast dropped too low, and wind conditions that sent his line looping in every direction but the one intended. By Alf's own admission, after two fishless weeks he "slid back" to his single-action casting outfit. "But only long enough to catch a few fish to see what it felt like," he added.

It took a while, but each time Alf used the fly rod his casting became a bit more proficient — and each time he learned a bit more about controlling the line in the air and in the water. Then everything came together when a steelhead finally latched onto a Pink Framus he was drifting through a run. Alf's conversion had started in earnest.

It has been several years since Alf took up the fly rod, and he now uses nothing else for steelhead. "I don't hook anywhere near the numbers that I did on bait or lures," he admitted recently, "but it's a lot more fun — and a lot more satisfying."

* * * *

Now Alf started his transition with a wealth of background knowledge about steelhead — important no matter how you elect to chase them — and he worked hard at developing and honing the skills required to attract them to his flies with a reasonable degree of consistency. One thing he didn't develop — and I hope never does — is a "holier than thou" attitude because he now fishes only with flies. There are already far too many snobs involved with fishing in general, and fly-fishing in particular.

It seems a quirk of human nature that when we become proficient at something, especially a purely recreational pastime like fishing, consistent success eventually leads to boredom. A successful angler who started out using an open-faced spinning reel might decide to try a free-spool casting model, thus creating new challenges and reviving flagging interest. Unfortunately, once the intricacies of the new equipment and techniques are mastered, there is a tendency to elevate one's self to a higher level in the pecking order which exists in the minds of some anglers. Suddenly, those who use "coffee grinders" are viewed in a condescending manner.

Anglers using rods of fibreglass are considered little more than cave dwellers by those using graphite — who in turn are snubbed by proponents of split cane. Steelheaders with new-generation Hardy Silex single-action casting reels are scorned by those who possess old Silex Superba models; however, true connoisseurs settle for nothing less than an antique Hardy Jewel or Major. Dry fly "purists" look down their collective noses at those who fish with streamers and nymphs, salmon moochers sneer at trollers, and so it goes. Much of this manifests itself as good-natured ribbing among friends, but there are some who take themselves — and the sport of fishing — far too seriously to have any "fun" at it. For them, fishing is a science to be studied, meditated over, theorized about, and pontificated upon in boring detail that is usually well peppered with Latin words. True, not all of these pompous zealots are fly-fishers, but if the truth be known, they certainly make up the majority.

Like most anglers with whom I associate on the water, I am AC/DC when it comes to fly-fishing. A few fishing friends who come to mind include Ralph Shaw, who delights in tempting trout with tiny Tom Thumb dry flies he ties by the hundreds each year. But when it comes to steelheading, he reaches for his well-used 10½-foot fibreglass drift rod with its Silex Superba reel. Ralph finds it challenging to cast with that outfit, and considers watching his bobber swim through a stretch of holding water a very interesting and exciting part of the pastime.

Barry Thornton's name is associated with the development and design of numerous West Coast saltwater fly patterns, but he is also skilled at luring chinook and coho salmon with drift jigs like Stingsildas, Pirkens and Buzz Bombs, which he fishes with a trout-weight spinning outfit. A fly rod is always there in his Boston Whaler, but it's reserved for periods when salmon are feeding near the surface. Otherwise, Barry "hunts" the shallows and drop-offs by watching the activity of sea birds; scanning the surface for leaping baitfish; judging the light conditions; and observing the tidal currents and wind conditions. There are no electronics involved — he does it all by sight and sense, which adds to the challenge and excitement.

Jack Shaw wrote two definitive best-sellers of interest to fly-fishers: *Fly-fish the Trout Lakes* and *Tying Flies for Trophy Trout*, but when he's fishing saltwater his fly rod is set aside in favour of a medium-weight mooching rod fitted with an Ambassadeur 6000 casting reel. With this outfit he fishes a selection of drift jigs or uses fresh bait, and while he doesn't turn up his nose at chinook and coho salmon, he would far rather concentrate on catching bottom fish. When a dinner-plate-sized flounder or chunky quillback rockfish swings over the gunwale, Jack is every bit as pleased with the results as when he slips the net under a trophy Kamloops trout.

These gentlemen share about 150 years of angling experience between them, most of it concerned with fly-fishing; however, they remain flexible enough in their thinking to vary their tackle and techniques when specific situations call for it. This improves their fishing efficiency but, just as important, it offers new challenges, fresh perspectives and increased interest, which all add up to a healthy injection of "fun."

WINTER STEELHEADING

What follows is instructional in nature, requiring reader participation. First, take a deep breath, then loudly scream "ha-a-a" for as long as necessary to totally expel all air from your lungs. Now, inhale while continuing to say "ha-a-a," which will probably sound more like a prolonged, wheezing drone. As your lungs fill to capacity, keep inhaling. I realize this sounds difficult, but it can be done and must be non-stop, so force yourself. Continue inhaling until your eyes protrude grotesquely from their sockets, the veins on your forehead bulge like knotted rope, and your heart begins pounding like the bass drum in a Royal Canadian Legion pipe band. As your knees buckle and you feel yourself blacking out, keep inhaling for just a few more seconds.

This exercise is known as "Terminal Inhalation" (TI), and your single, unbroken intake of breath should last for one full minute. If this sounds impossible, let me assure you that it is easy to accomplish by suddenly immersing your body in ice water, a common occurrence while fishing for winter-run steelhead. Often with brother and sister steelheaders serving as an appreciative audience.

Of various methods employed to achieve TI, a real crowd-pleaser for its stylish grace is the "Full-length Forward Flop" (3F). Wade out from shore into fairly slow-flowing water about two feet deep, then locate a rock with a flat top approximately the size of a dinner plate. The exposed part should be even with, or protrude slightly above, the surface. Step up on top of the rock and stand with both feet together, a posture which requires total concentration in order to maintain your balance while you cast.

When a fish suddenly hits, frantically sweep your rod upward, raising both arms quickly overhead in a useless attempt to pick up slack line and set the hook. This violent movement makes you teeter backward off balance, which you counteract by bending forward at the waist just as the departing fish snaps the line tight, thereby transforming your upraised rod into a highly efficient lever. Maintain your pose — feet firmly together, body now rigidly erect, arms fully extended overhead — while toppling forward like a falling tree, screaming "ha-a-a" in preparation for the next step.

Upon entering the water, immediately stand up or roll to one side as inhaling with your face submerged is not recommended — and at this point you will have started TI.

An even more entertaining performance for spectators is the exciting "Swift Water Acrobatic Pratfall" (SWAP). Unlike the 3F, the SWAP requires the type of white water which canoeists generally refer to as "life threatening." It need only be one foot deep, but the bottom should be paved with perfectly round, dead smooth rocks approximately the size of 10-pin bowling balls, each coated with algae having characteristics similar to Teflon.

Your waders should have well-worn rubber cleats rather than felt soles or aluminum studs, and you must avoid using a wading staff in order to windmill your free arm around like a one-bladed propeller as you jitterbug wildly, your feet a blur of water-spraying motion while you attempt to maintain your balance. Although this creates the appearance that you are dancing in place, you will actually be washing rapidly downstream. Finish your performance by screaming "ha-a-a" as you kick both feet up to eye level at the same time, flipping yourself backward into the river with your head and shoulders facing upstream. This last part is stressed so that despite the shallow depth, the current can force water inside your waders, billowing them out like the Goodyear blimp as you rocket downstream toward the raging rapids which immediately precede the high waterfall.

Unfortunately, space doesn't permit covering the multitude of other interesting, often exciting, methods anglers employ to totally immerse themselves in ice water. However, learning the 3F and SWAP will provide neophytes with some excellent insight into this often-overlooked component of winter steelheading.

THE SHAGGY COACHMAN

The burr in the uniformed commissionaire's voice had probably softened over the years he had spent in Canada, but there was more than enough left to denote his Northern England birthplace near the

Scottish border. We often met while working the graveyard shift at RCAF Station Comox. Dave Martin's job was to control access to one of the large hangars, mine was to service the CF-100 jet interceptors of 409 Squadron.

The only good points about working midnight shifts were that I could fish during weekdays when the rivers were uncrowded, and that slack periods at work provided opportunities to sit and yarn with Dave at his post on the flight line access door of No. 7 hangar. There, whenever time permitted, we chatted over countless cups of coffee and far too many cigarettes. Usually Dave talked and I listened. There were harrowing tales of life in the trenches during the First World War, and accounts of the years he spent as town constable in the coal-mining town of Cumberland, southwest of Comox. But mostly it was fishing talk, for Dave had experienced the peak of Vancouver Island's sport fishing.

One night during late summer, I entered the hangar and greeted Dave with a friendly insult. As usual, he blustered and growled about my lack of respect and insolence. "Don't be gettin' sassy, ye young whelp," he cautioned, wagging his finger at me. "I've brought ye a present — but if ye can't be civil ye'll bloody well do without."

"I'll be a good boy, Uncle David," I whimpered in a squeaky voice.

"Bah! I'll 'Uncle David' ye." He reached into a side pocket of his dark blue tunic and withdrew a white envelope. He opened it and shook four large streamer flies out onto the table top.

"Coachman bucktails," I said, picking one up.

"Aye, laddie, but these are special. These are tied by an old chap in Cumberland who never uses a vise. He does everything while holdin' the hook with his fingers. Take a close look and tell me what's different about it from a regular Coachman."

I studied it closely. "Well, it appears to be the hair from about half a deer's tail tied onto a 2/0 hook, but the most evident thing is the body: instead of wrapping the peacock herl around the shank, it looks like he's tied in little short pieces of it — in fact it looks a little bit like coarse chenille."

"Aye. And that's precisely what makes them so deadly — that big shaggy body. Big fly, big fish. Steelhead or cutthroat take these when nothing else will attract them."

"You sure these aren't bass flies?" I teased. "Or maybe pike? Hell, you'd need a derrick to throw them."

"I'll take the damned things back then!" he snapped, reaching for the three streamers still on the table.

My hand darted out and swept the flies away. "Oh, that's okay, Dave, I may break my poor old rod trying to throw them, but I'll give them a try."

"Well in that case shut yer mouth and pay attention," he commanded, "and I'll tell ye how to use them properly."

* * * *

In the early 1960s, a small run of summer steelhead ghosted through the Puntledge River near Courtenay. Few anglers paid them heed, for chinook and coho salmon had a much greater following during the summer and fall months. That suited me fine; I much preferred roaming the rivers to sitting in boats. Some of my favourite haunts on the Puntledge produced satisfying results, but one, the Barber's Pool, proved my nemesis. Although I worked the long, crescent-shaped pool faithfully with flies, lures and bait, it yielded nary a strike, let alone a fish. The steelhead were there, for while snorkelling its deep, slow-moving water on several occasions, I had watched silver-flanked forms cruise cautiously out of sight at my approach. All of which added to my frustration at continually drawing blanks over three seasons in a row.

Although Dave seldom fished the rivers any more, he was familiar with the Barber's Pool, and claimed it had treated him well over the years. While I listened politely and never disagreed with him, he could sense I remained unconvinced about the pool's productivity. I guess that was his reason for giving me the four Shaggy Coachman bucktails, along with some very explicit instructions on precisely how to use them.

Two days passed before I decided to fish the Puntledge. I arrived at the Barber's Pool to find another angler present — a great blue heron perched high on the branch of a dead snag overlooking the river. I selected a comfortable rock and sat down to observe the bird for a while. Perhaps because of my presence, the ungainly-looking creature stayed only a minute or so longer, then I was treated to the sight of its graceful take-off. The heron's huge wings moved slowly, almost lazily, but its departure was swift as it banked away, climbed to treetop level, then disappeared on its downstream journey.

I sat awhile, studying the pool: the water was "normal" for that time of year, meaning low. Most of the Puntledge flowed through a huge BC Hydro pipeline running parallel to the river. Fortunately, the three-mile stretch between the diversion dam and the power-generating station had several deep pools which offered fish a semblance of security and comfort. And, despite the pipeline's presence, that stretch of river remains one of the most scenic on Vancouver Island.

I heaved myself to my feet and picked my way over the jumble of rocks to the water's edge. Removing the Coachman's large hook from the keeper ring, I followed my mentor's directions to spit on the fly and work the saliva well into the hair wing and body. I then coated the entire length of the tapered leader with saliva. This, Dave assured me, would make the fly sink quickly. He had recommended a 12-foot leader, but I opted for nine feet out of deference to the fairly slow action of my fibreglass fly rod. The shorter the leader, the easier it would be to cast the big, heavy, hairy, air-resistant fly.

When I had drawn a sketch of the pool to refresh Dave's memory, he jabbed his forefinger right into its centre. "There! Ye want the still water right there — or as close to it as ye can get — to make this method work properly."

I positioned myself accordingly and started working out my line. Determining the aerodynamics and trajectory of the Shaggy Coachman took a while, but after a series of violent contortions that threatened permanent damage to my back and shoulders, I finally slapped it onto the water a reasonable distance from shore.

"Let it sink right onto the bottom," Dave had coached. "Give it about 20 seconds or so, then point the rod tip right down to the water. Reach up and grab the line right at the stripping guide and reef down — and at the same time lift the rod tip up to the 11 o'clock position." At this point he had stood up to pantomime the procedure, whereupon a passing aircraft technician asked if he was teaching me semaphore. Dave paused long enough to snarl a reply at the "young snot," then continued, "This pulls the fly forward about

10 feet all told. It travels through the water like a bullet — now it's there, now it's not."

"Okay. But why am I doing all this?"

"I'm gettin' around to that, ye impatient whelp! Now picture if ye can the steelhead lyin' on the bottom, just minding his own business. All of a sudden the fly lands on the surface and sinks down to the bottom. Now what do ye think that fish is goin' to do?" Before I could reply he continued, "He's not goin' to do anything — he's simply goin' to lie there and wonder what it is that fell into the water way up there in front of him. But then his curiosity will get the best of him and he'll finally decide to go take a look. And just about the time he gets there, or shortly thereafter, the fly suddenly disappears — whoosh!

"Well now, the fish was just curious up to this point, but now he's mad. Whatever it was he was looking at has suddenly up and got away. But ye've reefed in that 10 feet or so of line and then ye stopped and let the fly sink again. The fish sees the fly and takes off to investigate, but this time he's all tensed up. And this time when ye jerk that fly, it's not going to get more than a couple of feet before he has it."

"Will I always get a strike on the second pull?"

"No laddie," he cackled, "don't be daft. Many's the time ye'll never get a bite at all. But if the fish are within sight of the fly when it lands, ye'll probably get one — and normally on the second pull. But ye keep pulling and waiting until ye've got the fly right into shore. Then ye simply move up or down the pool and try again. Oh, laddie, I'll tell ye, ye've never felt a hard strike until ye've had a steelhead smack that fly. It'll almost tear your arm off."

I counted slowly to 20, then reached for the line and performed the first movement. Twenty seconds later I did the same — or started to. My left hand was about belt level, the rod shaft barely past horizontal, when a savage strike almost gave me heart failure. For a fraction of a second I envisioned the granddaddy of all steelhead, but the five-pounder rocketing into the air quickly dispelled that notion. It was a great to-do, as battles with super-charged summer steelhead usually are, but after the spunky hen trampolined all over the pool in a vain attempt to shed the hook, I finally led her into the shallows.

There I admired the faint blush of rose along her gill covers and lateral line, her olive back with its scattering of ebony spots, and her still lustrous white belly. She was sleek and graceful looking, her torpedo-shaped body tapering to the thick wrist and broad tail that makes this breed the strongest and gamest of freshwater fish. With the hook removed, she lost little time in heading back to the safety of the depths.

Two more fish eventually took my fly that day, but farther downstream. Both were slightly larger, but neither could match the thrill of my personal hoodoo pool's spell breaker.

* * * *

The Shaggy Coachman worked well on cutthroat trout in the brackish estuaries of various rivers and creeks; however, it wasn't necessary to use Dave's cast-wait-jerk procedure, for they usually smashed the large bucktails with wild abandon on normal hand-twist or stripped retrieves. While his retrieve works with other large patterns, the Shaggy Coachman outshines them all, perhaps because of its body construction. Being slightly iridescent, peacock herl reflects light, and in a ragged, irregular-shaped body these reflecting surfaces are multiplied and radiate minute flashes.

I have used this technique successfully throughout various regions of North America and Central Europe. While not a sure cure for trout-fishing doldrums, it occasionally produced rainbow, brown and brook trout when other tactics failed. Other anglers, having tried it, have also added it to their bag of tricks. If you decide to try Dave Martin's unorthodox method, remember the canny old fisherman's advice: First ye make them curious, then ye make them mad — then ye get ready for one hell of a strike.

SYMPATHY

"Ow! This has not been one of our greater days of steelhead fishing," said Big Bill as he shrugged out of his fishing vest.

"I believe the proper term is 'skunked'."

"That's right. Ow! Severely. Just like I happen to be severely hurtin' in my lower extremities, and I am severely thirsty — as in parched!" Peeling down his chest waders, Bill reached into his pocket and withdrew the keys to his Buick. Handing them to me he said, "You drive. I'm taking these damned boots off, then I'm going to sit in my sock feet and suffer in silence until we get to Fishermen's Lodge — and then I'm going to replace some of the body fluids that are rapidly draining from these blisters on my poor old tootsies. Ow!"

It wasn't until we had parked beside the Salmon River that Bill discovered he had forgotten his heavy woollen stockings. Although wearing only lightweight cotton socks, he decided to pull on his chest waders and fish, anyway. Bad move. We fished our way upstream over the rough, boulder-strewn river, and in less than a mile Bill had large blisters on each foot. We started back immediately, but by the time we reached the car they had broken open.

When I pulled into the pub parking lot an hour later, Bill's feet were so swollen he couldn't get them into his shoes, even with the laces removed. He finally opened the car door and carefully lowered his stockinged feet oh-so-slowly to the ground, then stood up. "Ow! Ooh! Damn!"

Since it was Saturday evening, the pub was packed and noisy. However, when Bill walked through the door, the interior grew strangely silent. Being six-foot-two and weighing 270 pounds is no big deal in an area noted for big, burly loggers and miners, and being shoeless probably wouldn't have attracted much attention, but he was yelping loudly with each step.

We made our way to an empty table, where Bill eased down into a chair with a loud sigh. Within seconds, Walter placed two glasses of draft beer on the table. "Start a tab?" he asked.

"Oo-o-o-o!..." Bill replied in a loud, high-pitched squeal, suddenly pushing his chair back and slamming it into an elderly gentleman sitting behind him.

"What the hell?..." demanded the senior, leaping to his feet, a large wet stain on his shirt front and beer dripping from his chin.

I calmly grabbed my beer and pushed back from the table in case Bill knocked it over.

"What's wrong, big fella'?" Walter asked, fearing Bill was having a seizure or a heart attack.

"Oo-oo-oo...." Bill crooned, his pursed lips forming a perfect O, voice quavering like a lovesick coyote serenading the moon. He had slid well down in his chair, his right leg extended rigidly forward.

Walter's face was almost touching Bill's. "What is it? What's wrong?"

"Oo-o-o-o...." Bill took a deep, ragged breath. "I've got a damned charley horse in my leg, and when I straightened it I kicked the table with my big toe."

The pub erupted with loud, sustained laughter, and while Bill took it all in reasonably good humour, he growled, "I've come to the conclusion you damned Canucks are the most unsympathetic people in the world."

Later, as we were leaving, Walter asked Bill if he would be back the following Saturday.

"I don't really know," he replied. "Why?"

"Well if you're coming, phone and let me know a couple of days ahead of time — that way I can get some posters printed and really draw a crowd."

MINOR DETAILS

Aside from occasional cases when a rank novice catches the largest or most fish during an outing, certain anglers consistently produce fish while everyone else is skunked or manages spasmodic success at best. Over the years, I have fished with quite a few "lucky" anglers, and have concluded they are neither "born fishermen" nor particularly skilled at handling their equipment — they simply pay attention to details....

A half-dozen steelheaders were working the long run — three below the cut bank where we stood, the others across the river on a gently sloping gravel bar. Crony and I surveyed the situation: everyone was using bobbers and fishing either fresh or imitation roe. While the pool's lower end was moderately crowded, there was plenty of room at the top — but only because it required some fancy wading to reach. Crony smiled. It was one of our favourite spots, and either one of us could probably have waded to it blindfolded. However, there was no competition between us that day; I was strictly an observer, sidelined by a badly damaged coccyx, commonly known and more easily pronounced as the "tailbone." The recovery period had involved four weeks of slo-o-w sitting down on the edge of a firm cushion, and then only after lo-o-ng consideration about whether or not any movement at all, including breathing, was really worth the pain and effort.

I was living, limping proof that fat, elderly anglers should pay attention to small details like a layer of wet leaves camouflaging a steep, smooth, slippery, clay bank. It had been my intention to get down to the river, but not quite so quickly. Frantic clawing and friction had stopped my hectic toboggan slide toward what appeared to be a certain swim, but the damage to my backside was done. My initial response was to lie there biting large chunks out of assorted rocks and pieces of driftwood, but eventually the excruciating pain settled down to merely excruciating throbbing. I then gave serious consideration to simply remaining where I lay, in hopes that a Search and Rescue team would locate me, and a helicopter would arrive to airlift me out. Eventually I decided I might live, then limped my way, oh-so-slowly, back to the van. The long way around, avoiding the clay bank. Finding a comfortable position in which to place my damaged derriere on the seat was impossible, and the rough goat trail I had to drive over in order to get back to the main road didn't help much, either. Which was why, a month later, I was merely observing rather than fishing.

As Crony waded upstream, I leaned against a suitable tree and watched the anglers working the pool — all of whom I recognized. "Anything happening?" I asked the closest fellow.

"Nothin'," he replied. "I've been here since seven this morning, and nobody's caught a thing." My watch indicated he had been there about eight hours. Dedicated, if nothing else.

Crony was using a 10½-foot graphite rod and a level-wind casting reel. No bobber — only a hook and a single sinker clinched about 20 inches up the main line. Shortly after he waded into position, I saw him baiting up with one of the large, frisky night-crawlers he stores in an earth-filled wooden box in his garage.

Crony studied the water for a few moments, then made a short quartering cast upstream — scarcely 30 feet. He was too far away for me to make out any details, but I knew he was watching his line with the intensity of a great blue heron preparing to spear a fish. I pictured his line tracking the worm's journey as the current swept it into a short, narrow slot that was virtually unfishable — except from where he stood. About halfway through that first drift, Crony's long rod lifted and arched, then the surface boiled as a deep-bodied steelhead rocketed away, hell-bent for saltwater in a series of porpoising leaps.

"Fish on!" I shouted, adrenalin pumping as though I was holding the rod. Heads snapped up, eyes gauged the situation, then a half-dozen bobbers swam shoreward.

That fish was indeed on — about 18 pounds of big, red-sided, extremely agitated buck steelhead. He raced by, porpoising several more times before reaching the glassy slick where the long pool dumped into the beginning of a quarter-mile stretch of rapids. By this time over 100 yards of line separated Crony and the fish, and his quarry seemed as good as gone, for once it was into the rapids there would be no stopping it. Then, for some inexplicable reason, just as it reached the lip and certain freedom, it swapped ends and powered upstream, right back to the stretch where it had been hooked.

Crony waded shoreward into some slack water, then settled down to slug it out. It wasn't easy, for that buck was strong and stubborn, with size and weight in its favour. However, Crony persevered, and finally led the fish close enough to tug the hook from its jaw. If anything, Crony was probably more in need of resuscitation than the steelhead, which promptly swam off with a sweep of his broad tail that threw a quart or so of water in the angler's face. At which I smiled and offered a silent prayer for that supercharged buck to find an equally large and rambunctious female with which to mate.

* * * *

Why did several well-equipped and knowledgeable anglers go fishless while Crony hit a steelhead immediately? Far be it from me to make a statement on a topic as mysterious as why fish — any fish — develop lockjaw at times. Possibly there simply weren't many, if any, steelhead in that easily-fished part of the main pool; maybe those present had been recently hooked on roe and were still wary. The problem with this theory is that steelhead often break off, then immediately bite the same type of bait within the same amount of time it takes an angler to re-rig and cast out again.

Based on my role as observer, I offer the following comments: For starters, Crony knew the entire pool quite well, and the underwater details of that hard-to-reach stretch very intimately. There had been a moderately heavy rain the previous day, which meant a fair number of earthworms had washed into the river. Now legions of armchair experts claim steelhead don't feed while in freshwater, but many of us have noticed they do indulge in a strange practice that involves the ingestion of worms (and other tidbits), after which they run them through their digestive tracts, then excrete the remains. Call this unusual behaviour what you will, they do a lot of it after a winter rain has washed a fresh supply of worms into the river. For this reason, Crony had used a bait that many steelheaders ignore.

In order to have maximum control of his drifts, Crony waded as close to the holding water as possible. He could have used a bobber — we often do in that stretch — but there are some water conditions when "tight-lining" simply works better. Crony had attended to a lot of seemingly minor details, but when added up I suspect the sum total made the difference between his catching that steelhead and simply joining the others for a day on the river — with plenty of fresh air but no fish.

A GLORY FISH

Those who fish seriously for steelhead consider it a challenging and exciting pastime. However, they would also point out that it can be mystifying, demoralizing and downright frustrating at times. Ask any knowledgeable, experienced steelheader who has worked a likely-looking run diligently yet fruitlessly, then watched an obvious neophyte blunder along behind and immediately hook a fish. It happens, but that's steelheading.

During the early 1960s, a recently arrived sergeant at RCAF Station Comox asked for my advice on getting started at steelheading. I suggested he buy a nine-foot, fibreglass spinning rod, and an open-faced spinning reel capable of holding 200 yards of 12-pound test line. "Don't scrimp on quality," I warned. "Get the best you can afford — good equipment lasts longer, so it's cheaper in the long run."

A short list of necessary bits and pieces was jotted down on a piece of paper: Nos. 4, 2, 1 and 1/0 hooks; small barrel swivels; lead sinkers; 15-yard spools of 8- and 10-pound test line for leaders and drop leaders. Below the list I made a simple line drawing. "Make your leaders about 18 to 20 inches long, and tie the drop leaders for your sinkers to the front eye of the swivel — that's so the bait doesn't twist the leader. Dig a couple of dozen big worms for bait and you're in business."

I flipped the paper and sketched a rough map to indicate a well-trampled stretch of the lower Puntledge River which flows through the northern outskirts of Courtenay. "These are runs and deep pools. Start at the top end and fish them downstream. Quarter your casts upstream and let the sinker bounce right along the bottom. You'll snag up and break off a lot, but you'll find winter steelhead on the bottom. If you feel anything — the least hesitation — set the hook. Most times it'll be a rock, but once in a while it won't. After two or three casts, move a couple of paces downstream and do it over again. That way you'll cover the entire run."

This all took place on a Friday. On the following Monday, the budding steelheader hunted me down to relate that he had done exactly as instructed. After purchasing his equipment on Saturday morning, he returned home, assembled everything, dug some worms, then headed for the river. There, on his fifth cast, he hooked and landed a mint-bright female steelhead weighing 19 pounds. Although I had caught hundreds of steelhead, my personal record at that time was 17 pounds. Joe had beaten it with his first fish, and needed only five casts.

"Pity," I said, shaking my head.

He looked puzzled. "Why do you say that?"

"Getting your 'glory fish' so soon. You'll probably never get another steelhead that big if you fish till you're 90."

As it turned out, Joe was badly bitten by the steelhead bug, so he kept returning to that same area. After paving the river bottom with lead sinkers, hooks and swivels, he had nothing to show for his effort except ruddy cheeks and chilblains. Deciding to try other rivers, he spent the remainder of the season chasing off to more Vancouver Island streams than I previously knew existed. He ended his first season with precisely one steelhead to his credit — the original 19-pounder. The following spring Joe took up golf, and never did go back to the rivers. Maybe he quit steelheading too soon, but I hear he's an excellent golfer.

SPRING TONIC

Early spring is a pleasant time to fish for steelhead in rivers and streams along the eastern shore of Vancouver Island. As days grow longer and temperatures warm, the river banks give birth to fresh sights, sounds and scents. If temperatures in the mountains are warm enough, snow melt will raise water levels in the rivers, and fishing conditions may range from good to excellent. As long as there isn't too much of a good thing, like warm weather and rain.

Conversely, if the weather stays cold, snow tends to remain locked in the mountains, and the rivers run as low and clear as during the dry summer months. Steelhead are seldom plentiful during such periods, for low water keeps all but a few impatient fish milling about near the river mouths, hesitant about leaving the ocean. Those venturing into the shallow streams are wary and nervous, difficult to approach, even more so to catch. Movement, even the shadow cast by a fine strand of nylon monofilament, usually sends them fleeing for cover, so we fish for them early in the morning, before the sun hits the water, or late in the evening, when it has dropped behind the treetops. The alternative, if one must fish during bright daylight hours, is to seek deep, dark pools that offer the steelhead protection and security.

* * * *

Crony and I have walked about two miles upstream from my van, and there are still two more miles to go before we turn and retrace our steps. As I trudge around a bend, I see my partner standing high above the ground on the rotting trunk of a long-fallen red cedar. He spots me, touches a finger to his lips, then points to the water below. I move off the faint trail and pick my way through the dense tangle of brush between us. Crawling up on the fallen giant, I climb stealthily along its ramp-like trunk to stand beside Crony.

It is mid-day in early April. With the sun hanging overhead, it is possible to see in perfect detail everything within the crystal waters below. The river bottom spreads before us like a vast tapestry of colours: delicate shades of rose, maroon, green, blue, grey, and brown, glistening white quartz, and jet black pieces of coal. Dry rocks lining the shore are identical colours, but dull in comparison, lacking the sheen and vibrancy of those illuminated by water and sunlight.

I spot the male steelhead immediately. A fine fish, especially for this small stream. Fifteen pounds at least. The water is so clear he appears suspended in mid-air. The sides of his deep body are still silver, but a faint blush of pink has started showing along his lateral lines and gill covers. His brown back is flecked with black and gold, the markings discernible even from where we stand, 20 feet above. A handsome creature — for the time being. Before long, his chrome mantle will turn bright crimson, then dull red as the spawning rites are performed. By the time they end, his well-muscled body will be gaunt and scarred, his fins ragged.

Depending on what Nature has in store, he might die; however, if he has the strength he might make it back to the ocean. If ... if he survives the effects of malnutrition; if fungus doesn't eat away the protective slime coating his body; if he evades the river otters, black bears and eagles; and if he doesn't run afoul of an angler who keeps even such emaciated fish "for the smoker." Now, though, he is alive. A fine trophy.

"Where's the hen?" I ask.

"Straight upstream, about 30 feet," Crony answers quietly. "Right up against the left side of that big rock."

I cup my hands around my polarized sunglasses and stare at the water, trying to make her materialize. There she is. "Damn! Crony, that is a big fish."

"Uh huh. I'd say we're looking at an honest 20-pounder."

I tear my eyes away from the fish. "You going to come back later and try for them?"

Crony chuckles and shakes his head. "No. I considered it, mind you — but I haven't the heart to break up such a loving couple. Think of the beautiful babies they'll be able to make if they manage to spawn. How about you — want to have a go at them?"

"Not me, sir. I'd rather take a chance on coming back in about four years and finding a whole school of 15- and 20-pounders instead of only two."

"Good! Let's make some more tracks then."

A half mile upstream, I find myself across the stream from Crony. A large, fallen maple lies parallel to the opposite bank, and another tree, a still-green fir, spans the pool's tail. "Bit dicey, eh?" I call over to my companion.

"Yeah. I can't do anything from this side. It looks fishy though — give it a try."

I adjust my bobber to suspend the pink, dime-sized, imitation roe of soft plastic at six feet. My cast is on target, the bait dropping scant inches from the maple. The small cigar-shaped bobber begins its downstream journey, hesitates ever so slightly, then plunges from sight. The tip of my long graphite rod lifts and I feel the surging power of a fish.

"Good man!" shouts Crony. "Big buck, about 11, 12 pounds."

The steelhead bulls his way downstream in a slow, determined run, and a feeling of helplessness overcomes me as he charges right into the toppled fir's submerged branches. There is nothing I can do to slow, let alone stop him, and I fear the fight has ended before really getting started.

Fate enjoys toying with anglers, for the slender strand of monofilament not only holds, it stays clear of the foliage. For no apparent reason, the buck then turns and charges back upstream, where the fight continues in the open water. It is mostly a series of powerful runs between the rocky jumble of shallow rapids at the pool's head, and the fallen fir at the tail. Not a spectacular battle — more a display of dogged, head-shaking resistance, punctuated with a run whenever the fish finds himself too close to shallow water.

He finally yields to the pressure of my rod and line, then wallows in the knee-deep water beside me. A big, red-sided male of 12 pounds or so, but despite his colour he is not yet ready to spawn. I use needle-nose pliers to pluck the barbless hook from his snout, then watch to see if he needs assistance. He lies quietly for a few moments, seems to realize he is once more free, then cruises slowly back toward deep water.

Crony picks up his rod, raises his arm in a casual wave, then wanders off upstream in search of a pool more to his liking. I reposition my plastic bait above the hook, then cast again toward the maple tree. The drift has barely started when it is intercepted by a bright hen about half the size of her predecessor. She races immediately for the pool's head, clears the water in a high, twisting leap, then streaks downstream toward the fir. My luck continues, for she turns just short of the submerged branches. A second jump, picture perfect, then another, and I giggle foolishly from sheer exuberance. Unlike the big, sulky male, her fight is fast and exciting, the sort that makes steelheaders notorious for telling tall tales — and causes outdoor writers to rack their brains for superlatives with which to describe the action. She, too, is eventually led into the shallows, where once more my pliers do their job. I am sure she will require resuscitation after such a performance, but she darts quickly away as the hook pulls free.

* * * *

As I recall, it was nearly a half-hour later when I finally followed Crony upstream. I had hooked four more steelhead, but Fate decided to frown on me. Three in a row were lost, two before I had a chance to see them. The one I did see was a bright hen — a big, beautiful fish, every bit as large as the released male. She treated me to a porpoising leap, then a high, head-shaking jump that rid her of the hook. The last fish was a buck of scarcely six pounds. A strong little fellow, but lacking the aerobatic zip of the female. Males are not normally ones to waste their strength with jumping — which means that while their fights often last longer, they seldom match those of the females for excitement.

Three fish landed and released, plus three more lost, was more than enough excitement for me that day, especially after seeing two steelhead that most of us can only dream of. Had I been fishing alone, I would have quit after releasing the small buck and called it a day. However, Crony was set on investigating what the upper stretches had to offer, so I trudged those extra three miles, for a total of eight, round trip. Great for my lungs and cardiovascular system, absolute hell on my flat feet. Crony fished ahead of me all the way, but for a change it was to no avail — he got nary a nudge for his efforts, let alone a definite bite. But that's steelheading — even when conditions are good, never mind during springtime, low-water conditions.

I was, of course, extremely sympathetic about my friend's run of bad luck, suggesting it was not really due to incompetence and lack of hand-to-eye co-ordination, but simply a sign of advancing age and excessive consumption of cheap alcohol. This might seem a bit unkind, but as the shoe was usually on the other foot, I simply took advantage of returning that which I usually receive. Crony simply bided his time until I finally ran down, then said, "Well, Jones, when I think about all the times you've gone fishless when the snow was blowin' horizontal to the water, or when your guides were iced up so bad you couldn't even cast, you have to admit that if you're gonna get skunked, this is the best time of the year to do it."

Ah yes, that Crony, such a wise man.

STEELHEADING EAST VS WEST

What happens when a western steelhead angler is plucked from remote surroundings beside a large, glacier-fed river and plunked down on a small Great Lakes tributary with shoulder-to-shoulder steelheaders? Or vice versa? Thanks to modern aviation, anglers from both regions can sample each others' fishing with relative ease. All it takes — aside from time and money — are a few adjustments in tackle, techniques and thinking. Permit me a few examples....

Several anglers are spaced along the left bank of Owen Sound's Sydenham River, some on shore, others in the water. A few have steelhead on the bank, but not many. Arnie Clark spots an opening and heads for it. His outfit consists of a nine-foot, lightweight rod, and a trout-weight spinning reel loaded with four-pound-test line. The small tackle box stowed in his jacket pocket is filled with a colourful collection of banana-shaped Flatfish and Quikfish plugs of various sizes. He selects a "Skunk" (black body with white stripes) and knots it carefully to his gossamer line.

Arnie wades stealthily into position at the head of a curving pool. A backhanded flip of his rod delivers the lightly-weighted lure across the stream, where it lands quietly then dives from sight. As the current causes the diving plug to swing downstream, Arnie moves his rod tip slowly to the left, increasing the lure's travel. When the line finally straightens, he moves the rod tip slowly to his right and the lure obediently follows. He continues these pendulum-like sweeps, occasionally releasing a bit of line from the spool, and his undulating lure effectively sweeps the bottom from side to side. While others about him chat and joke, Arnie remains alert to his rod tip and the line's position. Steelhead hitting a retrieved lure are notorious for almost tearing the rod from your hand, but when a little wobbling plug drops downstream toward them, they often mouth it gently, then spit it out. But not with Mr. Clark on the business end. He is like a coiled spring waiting to react at the first indication of a fish.

Less than five minutes into the exercise his rod flashes up in a handle-to-tip curve and 10 pounds of silver rockets across the surface in three low, greyhounding leaps. As the fish bores downstream, anglers reel in their lines, and those who are wading back-pedal toward shore. Arnie follows it to the next pool, yielding and retrieving line as necessary. The river is deep and fairly free of obstructions, so it's mostly a matter of utilizing his equipment's resilient strength to its utmost — and hoping the small hooks hold. Arnie knows the limitations of his tackle and works it hard.

His flexible rod absorbs much of the punishment, and his reel's drag remains smooth as silk. The runs grow shorter and weaker, then the deep-bodied fish finally rolls onto its side and is led over the rim of a large net wielded by a fellow angler who has offered to lend assistance.

* * * *

Crony has a soft spot for the Browns River, near his Comox Valley home. From high on Forbidden Plateau, it rushes and tumbles through high-walled, virtually impenetrable canyons to join the larger Puntledge River. Its lower reaches are a series of waterfalls and cataracts, with occasional deep pools, interspaced with shallow, swift-flowing water. As a result, steelhead seek cover wherever they can find it: tight against submerged rocks; beneath foaming carpets of white water; or in rock fissures scarcely large enough to conceal their bodies.

Crony uses a 12-foot rod with an ancient Silex Superba reel, and despite the clear water, his leaders are 15-pound test. At the first pool he studies the situation, then ponders soft-plastic egg imitations, yarn flies, or Spin 'n' Glo winged drifters. He finally selects a Spin 'n' Glo with a fluorescent orange body and white rubber wings. Suspended below a four-inch, torpedo-shaped bobber of foam plastic, it will be held close to the bottom by a heavy sinker.

Crony wades into position and makes a wide-swinging sidearm cast. Lure and bobber arc through the air and alight in perfect position to drift through a faintly visible cleft in the rock bottom. His bobber tilts and swims over the crack, a short drift covering only six feet. Nothing. He reels quickly for a moment, then free-spools line, allowing his lure to swim through another likely spot. As the bobber sweeps beside a submerged slab of sandstone it hesitates, then dips beneath the surface. Crony's long rod snaps upward and the fight is on.

The water is barely knee deep, so there is nowhere for the steelhead to go but up. Once, twice. High, twisting jumps. It races across the channel, churning the surface like a miniature speedboat, then veers downstream. Crony, rod tip raised, uses the palm of his hand to apply pressure to the reel's exposed rim. The fish gains a channel of fast water and is gone. The reel's ratchet sets up a droning wail as Crony charges downstream, slipping, sliding, and kicking spray shoulder high. Large boulders are strewn along the channel, and that crazy fish runs a zigzagging course through most of them. Crony's line saws and grates against the rocks until he is able to wade out, then reach around each boulder with the rod tip to clear it.

Over 100 yards downstream he finally regains control and leads a hen steelhead into the shallows. We admire her silver perfection, argue amiably about her weight, then agree that 10 pounds wouldn't stretch the truth too much. The barbless single hook is tugged free and she is gone in a flash. Crony sits down on a handy rock and checks his line. The leader is fine, but his 25-pound-test main line is badly scuffed and frayed along much of its length. Light line? Not on that river.

* * * *

Although Arnie's lightweight gear worked well on that small Ontario stream, it would be virtually useless on most large western rivers. Conversely, Crony's heavy tackle, necessary for handling fish in strong-flowing, obstruction-littered currents, would frighten most self-respecting Ontario steelhead back into the Great Lakes. However, while their tackle and techniques differ in many ways, their approach to fishing for steelhead has many similarities: they know their rivers and how to read the water; they are intimate with the habits and preferences of steelhead; their tackle is in top-notch condition; they pay attention to details like using line of good quality, making sure knots are properly formed, and that hook points are always sticky sharp; and both keep well-detailed diaries, which are far more dependable than memories when it comes to recalling details over the years. If anglers like Crony and Arnie suddenly switched places on their favourite rivers, there might be a bit of initial head scratching while things were sorted out, but if there were steelhead present, a few of them would probably be in serious trouble before day's end.

THE FLOORSHOW

I wander downstream and find Crony fishing the lower end of the long, sandy-bottomed Farm Pool.

"Anything doing?" I ask.

"Nope. Worked it from the top end right on down. Nary a sniff. How 'bout you?"

"Nothing." I sit on a piece of driftwood and watch my companion work the waters with his long rod and single-action reel. Each cast sends his torpedo-shaped cork bobber and roe-baited hook well upstream, landing close against the steep bank where the channel is deepest. Although it is the tag end of April, we are hoping to encounter a few late-running steelhead.

We realize that our chances of catching anything are similar to winning a lottery or being struck by lightning, but hope is what keeps most of us fishing, especially for steelhead.

A few minutes later, Crony turns and wades ashore. "You give up on that buggy whip?" he asks.

"Not likely. Just waiting for you to quit hogging all the good water so I can cast without ripping your ear off."

"Good!" He shrugs out of his heavily-laden canvas vest. "You can entertain me while I eat my lunch."

I wade into position and start casting. There is nothing very graceful about chucking a 30-foot shooting head that sinks like a strand of baling wire when it hits the water. If you watch an experienced angler casting with a floating, double-taper line, you see rhythmic, fluid grace. A winter steelheader using a shooting head with monofilament running line works both arms like opposing pistons, double-hauling the airborne head to speed it up, then shoot it forward. One's entire body goes into the effort, and while there is certainly rhythm involved, it's machine-like rather than graceful.

My first cast quarters well upstream, allowing the fly to drift past about 20 feet in front of me as I strip in line. Nothing. I extend the second cast about two feet, and the third. The idea is to sweep the bottom from my side to the opposite bank. I'm not really expecting anything more than a bit of casting practice after Crony has worked the pool so thoroughly with fresh bait, which is why I almost go into cardiac arrest at the sudden, violent strike.

Over 50 years of experience as an angler develops automatic, finely-tuned reflexes. Without conscious thought I raise my rod tip to tighten the slack line, calmly place my right heel on top of my left toe, then step backward. Fortunately, as I start toppling my feet untangle, so I back-pedal madly and barely catch my balance. The fish is now racing away at an alarming rate of speed, so I quickly step forward to relieve pressure on the leader, tripping in the process. Pitching forward, I stagger frantically ahead for several spray-tossing steps, my upper body parallel to the surface, then mush to a halt in chest-deep water. There are no further problems other than excruciating pain from various internal organs that feel like they might have torn loose.

"Way to go!" Crony whoops. "Run it down and kick it to death!"

My opponent is about eight pounds of bright-silver buck. The tussle lasts a few more minutes, then I draw him close enough to reach the barbless fly with my needle-nose pliers.

"What you get it on?" Crony asks as I wade ashore.

"Squamish Poacher." I show him the bright orange shrimp pattern.

"You should have kept that fish," my friend says accusingly.

"How so?"

"If it turned up its nose at fresh roe for a fly that looks like a cooked shrimp swimming around in freshwater, it was clearly bent on suicide. You'd have been doing it a favour."

§FOUR
PERIPHERAL VISIONS

DIVING DIPPERS

When friends from Ontario said they wanted to see and photo-graph American dippers while visiting Vancouver Island, I promptly suggested the Qualicum River Salmon Hatchery. "They nest right under the diversion dam spillway," I explained, "so you can get fairly close to them."

Thus, one early April day, two tripod-mounted cameras were perched on the dam's walkway, the strong lenses of each aimed at a converging point on the rocky shoreline. Every few minutes a short-tailed, slate-grey bird made its way upstream, the bright silver body of a salmon fry gripped crosswise in its beak. The dipper's flight was erratic but predictable as it flitted from rock to rock, pausing on each to perform a few of its characteristic deep knee-bends and study its surroundings. Its final stop before disappearing under the walkway was always the very rock at which my friends' cameras were trained.

After a half-hour or so, a rather hefty, gruff-looking hatchery worker approached, a puzzled expression on his face. "What's up?" he asked.

"Dippers," I replied.

His frown transformed into a grin. "You ever heard them sing?"

I smiled and nodded. "Yeah — when I'm fishing steelhead."

"Haven't they got just the sweetest song?" the big man said. "I class them right up there with meadowlarks."

I agreed, stating they sang every bit as beautifully as the nightingales I used to hear in Germany (usually while eel fishing at night). My friends seemed mildly amused at the fact two grown men were unabashedly gushing over the singing attributes of such a nondescript-looking bird — but they had never heard one sing.

Most folks have favourite birds, the species usually depending on where they happen to live, or, perhaps, through a memory of some past incident or pleasant time of life. That those I favour tend to be found on or near the rivers of British Columbia can probably be attributed to a rather questionable lifetime spent observing nature over the tip of a fishing rod.

Some birds seem so much a part of the scene around us they receive little more than casual glances as we go about our business, while others are so rarely seen their presence causes finger-pointing excitement and admiration. Bald eagles are common on Vancouver Island, but the sight of one soaring overhead or simply sitting in a tree still draws my attention. So do feisty old ravens peering solemnly from the branch of a dead cedar; rowdy crows cartwheeling through the skies, performing aerobatics that turn human pilots green with envy; the swift, swooping flight and staccato call of a kingfisher; and great blue herons — those contradictions of gawkiness and grace — as they slowly stalk the shallows in search of unsuspecting fish and frogs. However, when all is said and done, the birds that really activate my admittedly underdeveloped Audubonish tendencies are dippers, which I see virtually every time I fish one of our western streams.

No matter how interesting or demanding the fishing might be, a dipper's buzzing flight causes everything to cease while I watch its performance. What other songbird can entertain you by flitting into the water almost at your feet, then diving beneath the surface to walk busily along the bottom searching for aquatic nymphs, larvae and small fish? And if the surface is relatively calm and clear, you might even see it flap its stubby wings to seemingly "fly" underwater as it goes about its business. Then, if its search is successful, it bobs to the surface and hops onto a nearby rock, and almost always goes into the knee-bending dance routine that gave the bird its common name.

Perhaps, if you are lucky, when the dance ends the air will fill with a warbling song so sweet and pure you will be hard pressed to believe it is coming from such a drab-looking little bird. An ornithologist or birder might explain that the dipper is simply staking its territorial claim. Perhaps. But I like to think they are, in fact, reincarnations of great opera singers — Caruso and Melchior, Trauble and Callas — and they sing because they recognize an appreciative audience.

Most ornithologists class dippers as descendant from wren-like forebears, but some argue in favour of thrush ancestry. Whichever, they are one of nature's marvels, so well adapted to their environment and habitat that nothing imaginable is required to improve their lifestyle. Well, maybe one thing: for aquatic birds dippers are lousy swimmers. Eager, but inefficient. Rather than being webbed, their feet are typical of perching birds; thus, while they are swimming along the surface their progress is slow and jerky, often assisted with sporadic flapping of wings. Once submerged, however, their performance improves amazingly.

The buoyant bird's unusual ability to walk on river bottoms is based on the same principle as the diving planes on a submarine. By tilting the leading edges of their wings, they control the flow of water over them. Increasing their wing angle downward creates more water pressure to hold them on bottom.

Four notable evolutionary modifications have helped dippers adapt to life in and out of the water: a thick layer of true down underfeathers protects them from icy water and freezing temperatures, and an extremely large oil gland effectively waterproofs their feathers. In fact, this preening gland is 10 times larger than those found in similar-sized songbirds like starlings. A moveable flap of skin over their nostrils prevents water from entering their breathing passages while submerged, and a nictitating (third) eyelid protects their eyes.

The nest construction of dippers is truly unique. I have one in my possession — the victim of a bridge reconstruction, it was carefully removed and passed on to me. It is hemispherical, 10 inches high, eight inches wide, and six inches thick. A circular entrance hole about two inches in diameter is located slightly to the left of centre on the front. It leads into a spherical, grass-lined chamber approximately four inches in diameter. Green moss forms the bulk of the structure, but long pieces of slender roots are woven lengthwise through the spongy mass, apparently to give it tensile strength. It is not only a comfortable-looking nest, it even has a roof over it.

Dipper nests are situated near water, presumably in order to keep the outer shell moist and resilient. They are commonly found tucked behind the face of a waterfall or dam spillway, for such locations keep the nests well dampened and offer excellent protection from predators. If sites like these are not available, dippers will use virtually anything that is handy: the roots of a tree overhanging a cut bank; a crevice or crack along the face of a cliff; even structural supports under bridges or wharfs. In such cases nests are kept moist by the dippers flitting back and forth between river and nest, then shaking water from their feathers to dampen the mossy outer shell.

Dippers may breed up to three times a year, but twice is more the norm. The courting ritual is similar to other perching birds — meaning the male struts pompously around a seemingly disinterested female and makes a complete fool of himself (which sounds suspiciously similar to human courting rituals). One practice I have observed on several occasions is what I assume to be the male bird flashing signals to the love of his life with the nictitating membranes over his eyes. These tiny circles of white are quite noticeable, even at distances of 100 feet or so. Displays last up to a minute, during which time the signalling bird ceases dipping and bobbing, and concentrates on sending what appear to be semaphore messages of mad passion.

Egg clutches range from three to seven, but the average is four or five. The female incubates the tiny white eggs for 16 days while her chauvinistic husband flits about leading the good life, no doubt getting even for having had to play the fool to attract her attention in the first place. Once the young hatch, he might condescend to help out occasionally with some of the household and feeding chores — but not very often.

One of the rivers I fish has a fairly high waterfall. I once noticed a dipper flying in and out of the spray billowing from one corner of the cascading water. I waded across the river, pulled the collar of my raincoat snug around my neck, then thrust my head under the spray. The dome-shaped nest was scarcely a foot from my face, and through its circular opening I saw four chicks. The feathers atop their heads stood out like the spiked hairdos of a heavy metal rock band, and eight tiny black eyes stared back at me for just a moment before their bright yellow beaks opened. Having nothing to offer them, I backed away from the waterfall and let their mother get back to her task of feeding them.

After two or three weeks the young are ready to leave their nest. Absolutely fearless, they show no hesitation at leaping into the water, nor do they require lessons in swimming, diving, walking on the bottom, or any of the other antics and feats that mark them as dippers — they appear to do everything by natural instinct.

For years I assumed the only predators dippers had to contend with might be raptors, weasels and mink. However, a fellow told me that while cleaning a 14-pound steelhead caught in the Browns River, he found in its stomach a small, grey bird he thought might have been a dipper. After asking around, I heard of two more instances where large steelhead had consumed birds, both definitely identified as dippers. This being the case, dippers frequenting Interior streams with populations of large, rapacious bull trout probably fall prey to them on occasion.

I have heard dippers called water wrens, water witches and water ouzels — the last of which is actually the British name for the closely related common dipper of Europe and Eurasia. However, Big Bill Jesse, my long-time fishing companion from Illinois, gave them what I think to be a most appropriate name. After observing their deep-knee-bending antics during a day of fishing, he dubbed them "those little, grey, teeter-ass birds."

No matter what you call them, should you find yourself walking beside a western stream, take time to look for a dipper. If you see one, stop to watch. The performance of these friendly little birds is guaranteed to brighten the drabbest of days. And if you are treated to an enchanting aria or two, consider yourself twice-blessed — you will be serenaded by one of the world's most beautiful and charming singers — and surely one of its most unique creatures.

SOMETHING TO CROW ABOUT

Vera called and told me to look out our living-room window. Neighbours were landscaping across the street, and a four-foot-high mound of topsoil lay in one corner of their yard. A crow perched on top of the pile appeared to be sunning itself. However, it was about to be disturbed, for approaching slowly from the side was a neighbourhood cat.

"It'll wait till the last minute and fly away," I prophesied.

"I don't think so," Vera replied. "He's been around for the past two days, and I don't think he can fly."

The orange tabby inched slowly to the base of the mound, and was just close enough to pounce when the crow suddenly emitted a high-pitched squawk and leaped straight at the cat, landing inches from its nose. The feline recoiled in surprise as the crow pressed the attack, repeatedly hopping into the air, and loudly cussing out the cat. Don't scoff. Crows are quite proficient at hurling obscenities when their dander is up.

The shocked cat continued backing up, then turned and scrambled for cover. Feathers still ruffled, the crow paced back and forth a few times, then, satisfied there would be no further interruptions, strode back up on top of the mound to continue its sunbathing.

This was our introduction to the crow Vera decided to call "Tennessee" because he walked everywhere. Please understand that we are of an age to recall a popular 1960s song called "The Tennessee Bird Walk," ergo, the crow's name. His gender was decided because, according to Vera, "He walks just like an old man — with his hands clasped behind his back."

We saw that grounded crow almost daily throughout the remainder of the summer, and he was always on foot. He was easily identified among other crows because his right wing tip was lower than the left, and he favoured our back yard because of the tidbits

Vera left there for him. If a flock of crows landed to rummage through the large field behind our house, Tennessee usually walked slowly and patiently toward them. Often the crows flew away before his arrival, but if he made it, he was accepted without incident.

One evening after a particularly hot day spent coho fishing off Comox, Larry DesChene and I were busy replacing lost perspiration with cold beer as we awaited a call to the supper table. Tennessee appeared, exploring the edge of our garden. As he poked about for tidbits, I said, "Let's try to catch him."

"Why?" asked Larry.

"Curiosity. Maybe his wing can be repaired."

"Well, I've got my landing net in the truck...."

"And mine's in the basement...."

Now anyone observing two adult, beery-breathed males racing about an open field with salmon-sized landing nets might rightfully suggest reservations be made immediately at some quiet retreat with barred windows and well-padded rooms. However, we honestly thought that with two of us outmanoeuvreing the crow, his capture would take little effort. The only problem was, Tennessee demonstrated that at least three months of practice had given him the ability to cover ground at a pace which would have shamed a roadrunner — and that he could cuss out humans with even more vehemence than cats.

Eventually Larry herded him toward centre field, then rushed him. Tennessee ran for it, but Larry started gaining on him. However, just as the net was about to engulf the fleeing crow, he spread his wings and started beating them. Tennessee rose quickly into the air and glided to a perfect landing well up in the branches of a poplar — never once missing or even slowing down his endless string of crow cussing.

"That bird isn't crippled," Larry panted in a raspy, accusing tone. "He only flies when he feels like it."

Tennessee stayed throughout the short Vancouver Island winter, but when the trees started budding in March he disappeared. Vera maintains that he probably walked north, seeking some quiet, peaceful place devoid of cats and demented humans with landing nets.

* * * *

Like coyotes, crows are seldom contemplated by folks who have nothing to do with them, and usually despised by those who do. Few farmers or gardeners are enamoured of them, especially if corn is their main crop. Even birders, those stalwart lovers of most things feathered, draw the line at crows, totally ignoring their good points to dwell on the fact that crows often steal the eggs of songbirds and eat their fledglings. The truth is, on most days crows are not busy raiding farm fields or bird nests; they are elsewhere, eating about a third of their weight in insects, spiders, slugs, mice and moles — few of which are welcome around houses or gardens.

Over the years crows have plundered my garden; stolen assorted articles (none of any possible use to them); awakened me at inhumane hours of the morning; eaten a small toad Vera considered a garden pet; and turned one of our cats into a craven coward. I am a confirmed dog man, but as cats go Snowball was acceptable. Named for her long, pure-white hair, she was friendly, scrupulously clean, and gentle with children. And, unlike most cats we have owned, she acknowledged me as part of the family.

One morning I let Snowball out of the house, then busied myself with the coffee pot. As the kettle heated I happened to glance out the window and noticed her creeping across the front yard, intently stalking an obviously injured crow. The pathetic-looking creature dragged one wing on the grass, and its head drooped as it staggered weakly and aimlessly around the lawn. The strange thing was, although that poor, bedraggled bird seemed totally unaware of Snowball, the gap never closed between them despite her patient stalking. For each inch forward the cat crept, the crow tottered an equal distance away.

The drama continued for several minutes until, finally, her attempts at stealth thwarted, Snowball suddenly lost control and charged. As the space between them narrowed, the crow leaped into the air and flew quickly up to the telephone line leading to our bungalow. There it landed, then slowly toppled forward to dangle upside down, wings askew, while it chuckled and chortled gleefully at its adversary. Now completely unstrung, Snowball began leaping repeatedly at the jeering crow, and in so doing failed to notice the black shape rocketing silently across the lawn from behind. Just as the second crow hurtled past, scant inches overhead, it cawed once — loudly. Snowball became a blur of white motion as she cartwheeled sideways and scuttled for safety beneath our ancient station wagon. As the "sick" crow flapped its wings a few times and righted itself on the telephone wire, the sneak attacker circled tightly, then flared its wings and landed beside its companion. They perched there for a few moments longer, chuckling and chortling to each other as only crows can, then flew off, probably seeking another cat to torment.

When it came time for me to leave for work, Snowball had failed to appear. I went out to the car, crouched down, and saw her cowering beneath the engine. It took a while, but I finally coaxed our still wild-eyed pet out and into the house. Thanks to various leaky oil seals, her back was streaked with black, giving her a slightly skunk-like appearance. It was a condition Vera and I became used to, for Snowball never fully recovered. From then on, if our shell-shocked cat happened to be outside when a crow flew over, she took immediate shelter under the closest vehicle.

* * * *

Over the years I have observed a few things about crows: they are selective, preferring only the ripest and most perfect of garden-grown berries and fruit; one should never leave shiny fishing lures, small tools, loose change or jewellery lying exposed about the yard or camp site; if crows were dedicated worm hunters, robins would starve to death because of their late sleeping habits; they are omnivorous, with eating preferences similar to vultures, sea gulls and garbage compactors; and, as proved by poor Snowball, they possess a diabolical sense of humour.

Crows are thrifty, too, often hiding food during periods of plenty so it can be eaten when pickings are slim. A few years ago, while I was salmon fishing at Toba Inlet with Big Bill Jesse and Peter Melwood, we tied our boat to a logging company raft so we could eat lunch. When Bill casually tossed his sandwich crust overboard, onto the water, a crow launched itself from the steep face of a nearby bank. It soared past the floating crust, executed a tight turn to the right, then swooped down and used its beak to pluck the crust from the surface.

A few wingbeats carried it upward onto the slope, where the crust was quickly buried under a layer of leaves and moss. Its job done, the crow flew back to its vantage point to watch for more goodies.

Pete could have tossed his crust onto the raft, but lobbed it into the water. After a repeat performance of picking up the crust and concealing it, the crow returned to its perch. It was my turn, so I flicked out my crust and the crow went into its aerial routine. Unfortunately, it made a miscalculation on its final approach toward the floating morsel, dumping itself into the water. Frantically flapping its wings against the surface, the bird headed for shore, about 15 feet away, which took it about 20 seconds or so. It appeared quite waterlogged as it stumbled ashore, where, after a thorough shaking and much ruffling of feathers, it decided against flying and climbed slowly up to its perch. Quietly, too, perhaps out of embarrassment. It was the only time I ever recall a crow being stuck for words.

FLY-FISHING

Folks with unusual abilities are all around us: they can find water by "dowsing" with forked sticks; foretell the future; hypnotize people; open childproof pill containers; refold road maps.... In my case it's levitation. That's right, the ability to physically elevate my body and move between two points, often over considerable distances. Unfortunately, I can't do this on command — it is strictly an involuntary phenomenon — nor can I recall any details that occur during the actual flight.

I became aware of my gift several years ago while leaping over a shallow creek, a tributary to the Tsolum River. About five feet wide, it was an easy jump, even in chest waders, so I jogged the last few paces to gain speed, then leaped. I was in mid-jump, right leg fully extended in front, left leg to the rear, when a violent eruption suddenly occurred in the water directly beneath my crotch.

"How in hell did you do that?" Gino McClean demanded as I walked back down the trail toward him.

"Do what?"

"Turn around and come back without landing on the other side! You were still a foot off the ground when you went past me."

"Never mind that," I said. "What in hell's in there?"

"Just those crazy coho. I swear they'll swim on wet grass if they think there's a place to spawn. You really scared them."

"I scared them?..."

And that's when it started.

My longest and highest flight occurred while I was taking a short-cut through a clearcut area overgrown with scrub alder about six feet high. With no trail to follow, I was going by dead reckoning. I stopped to listen for running water, then finally determined it was still at least 100 yards away. Just then I heard a loud scratching sound. Puzzled, I looked around. There was a lone fir tree about 50 feet away, and up its trunk were clambering two of the cutest little black bear cubs imaginable. The next thing I recall is standing waist-deep in the river. It was actually a stretch of quick-flowing rapids, which greatly assisted me in some extremely fast wading over a long distance downstream before I finally slowed down to catch my breath.

Thus far, my most memorable flight occurred while I was prospecting for October coho on a small river. The trail upstream meandered through a typical cedar swamp: tangles of salmonberry and huckleberry bushes, tall ferns, devil's club, and towering ever-greens that blocked out most sunlight. Upon reaching the turn-off to an often productive run, I ducked beneath the overhanging branches of a large red cedar, then waddled forward, my upper body parallel to the ground. I was just stepping down onto the sandbar when something moved about a foot below my descending boot. It was a large coho — still flopping, and missing a fist-sized chunk of flesh from its left side. My foot never got any closer to it.

The distance from there to the centre of the river was only 50 feet, but my route was right through the tangle of red cedar branches. My face was scratched as if by coarse sandpaper, and I was still humped over like a toppled letter L when I landed in the water. I lurched quickly to the far shore, then started searching for the bear I had obviously disturbed in mid-meal. Nothing. Anywhere.

As I had taken on water, I shucked my vest and undid my wader suspenders. I was bent over, waders down around my knees, when I noticed that the sand where I stood was covered with overlapping bear tracks of several different sizes. At this moment a small rock broke free from the high bank behind me and clattered noisily down to the shoreline. I eventually waded back to shore, drained my now thoroughly filled waders, then headed downstream, keeping well to the middle. After two flights in one day, I didn't need any more surprises.

MONSTER MAYHEM

It is blast-furnace hot on the exposed, crescent-shaped expanse of sand, but Chuck Cronmiller is sprawled on a folding lawn chair, obviously dozing. A few feet away, angling up from a sand spike rod holder, the shaft of his long rod bows toward the muddy Fraser River, its tip rhythmically pulsating in time with the surging current. I happen to be looking right at the rod when it is suddenly pulled violently downward, and the tiny brass bell tied to its tip jangles. The lawn chair goes flying as Chuck becomes instantly mobile. He reaches his rod just as the holder topples forward, uprooted from the sand by the power of one of the world's oldest and largest freshwater fish: a white sturgeon.

Chuck grabs the rod handle with both hands, raises its tip and jams the butt against his thigh. As line peels from the big Peetz single-action reel, he uses the palm of his hand to apply pressure to the outer rim, but to no avail. Spreading his feet and planting them firmly in the sand, he increases the pressure and leans well back on the rod. Eighty-pound-test monofilament hums like a hydro wire as his rod tip is slowly pulled lower and lower, and we watch in amazement as slowly, relentlessly, Chuck is hauled erect. Suddenly off balance, he staggers toward the water, his rod tip pointing directly at the departing fish. About the time I figure he is going for a swim, there is a sharp crack.

Bryan Wilson turns to Clarence McIvor, his guiding partner. "What did that remind you of?"

"A Road Runner and the Coyote cartoon?"

"Well, that too, I suppose. I was thinking of that fish Mike Wells got a couple of weeks ago. It hit and ran the same way."

"That's right. Pulled out the sand spike, too. But at least Mike got his fish in."

Chuck reels in the slack line. "That felt pretty big. Any idea what size?"

"Obviously bigger than you are," Clarence replies. "Seven, eight feet — maybe more. If you insist on 'releasing' them before we even see them, we'll never know."

Chuck grins. "I didn't really have much choice in the matter." He looks at the rest of us. "By the way, gentlemen, just in case you didn't notice, that was fish number five!" He splays his fingers and thumb for emphasis. "I'll be giving a seminar on sturgeon-fishing techniques later this evening on the patio. I'd advise you all to be there, and be prepared to take notes."

Good taste does not permit reporting the vulgar replies to his announcement. Four of us were on the charter: Chuck and Frank Gavin, both old friends from my air force days, and Jack Whelan, a fellow outdoor writer. Despite our having four identical baits in the water throughout the day, Chuck's had been the only ones to attract attention, a point he was not letting go unnoticed.

Mike Wells's big sturgeon was precisely our reason for being there. Two weeks earlier I had tagged along with Bryan and Clarence on a sturgeon charter involving six anglers. Our first stop had been downstream from Lillooet at Rattlesnake Point, a huge backwater with an excellent track record for productivity. Shortly after we beached our two boats on its curving tract of sand, each of the anglers had his lines in the water. Sturgeon fishing is often a game of hurry up and wait, but it was only 20 minutes later when the bell on Rudy Roman's rod sounded. His hoped-for monster quickly proved to be a fairly "small" fish of 52 inches, which put up a respectable fight against his heavy tackle.

Fifteen minutes later, Mike Wells's rod suddenly jerked down so forcefully the sand spike ripped free, spewing sand into the air. Mike made a desperate grab for the handle, virtually catching it in midair, then lurched toward the shoreline as the fish bored downstream.

Finally recovering his balance, he straddled the rod's long handle, then started fighting a fish larger than himself. It was a long, dogged battle, and the guides stood by with the motor idling on one boat in case the sturgeon left the pool. However, each time it seemed ready to run into the fast water, Mike managed to turn it. Over 40 minutes passed before the sturgeon was finally close enough for Clarence to slip a rope noose over its tail. Nearly seven feet long, it weighed 250 pounds, and was later divided up among the anglers.

After returning home to Courtenay, I showed colour slides of the sturgeon charter to my friends. As a result, a trip was hastily booked for the following week. Thoughts of catching fish larger than yourself has that sort of effect on many anglers.

* * * *

The lower Fraser is wide and open, but north of Hope it changes dramatically. There the Cascade Mountains compress it between steep rock walls, forming white-capped rapids, deep pools, and churning back eddies. Each sand-bottomed pool and stream mouth offers potential sturgeon water, but the rugged terrain makes access difficult, except by boat.

One hundred miles beyond Hope lies Lillooet, a picturesque town harking back to the Cariboo gold rush. It is now the prosperous centre for a sprawling community comprised of cattle ranches, vegetable and fruit farms, and a thriving lumber industry.

Lillooet was also headquarters for Fraser River Sturgeon Charters, the brain child of two fishing partners who decided to pool their knowledge and expertise by starting the business. At the time, Bryan Wilson was principal of the town's elementary school, and Clarence McIvor owned a feed store.

They used two sturdy, welded-aluminum boats: a 21-footer with a 200 h.p. outboard, and an 18-footer with twin 25s. As part of their fishing package, they provided 11-foot-long fibreglass rods, some with Penn multipliers, others with large Peetz single-action reels fashioned from mahogany and brass. The Penns were loaded with 60-pound-test monofilament, the Peetzes with 80.

Leaders were formed with braided Dacron, which is softer and more flexible than heavy monofilament. As sturgeon are scent feeders, visibility is not considered a factor. Typical baits included fresh sockeye salmon flesh, salmon roe, and large night crawlers. Depending on the type and size of bait used, hooks varied from No. 5/0 to 10/0. Used railroad spikes weighing about one pound served as sinkers. A drop leader of cotton string was used to tie them to a free-sliding swivel on the main line. This permitted fish to mouth the bait without feeling the sinker's weight; then once a fish was hooked, or if the sinker snagged on bottom, the string broke easily.

While travelling downstream to remote sandbars, we passed open cattle ranges, dense stands of jack pine, towering canyons of mineral-streaked sandstone, weather-sculpted banks of loose sand, and rocky gravel bars, some still populated by placer gold-mining operations. Black bear and mule deer sightings were common.

The guides actively promoted catch-and-release, a practice most anglers gladly accepted. Of the sturgeon caught during their four-month season, about 90% were released. The few retained for eating were usually juveniles — sexually immature fish in the four-to five-foot range. Each released sturgeon was measured and identified with a serial-numbered spaghetti tag in the dorsal fin, then its data were recorded in a book and periodically forwarded to the provincial fisheries branch. Their records included fish ranging in size from 18 inches to 10 feet, indicating that stocks were reproducing well.

* * * *

At each sandbar the boats were beached and unloaded; then, after spacing sand spikes along the shoreline, our guides rigged the terminal gear. Baits were large, often fist-sized, weighing up to a half pound. Smaller baits also worked, but with squawfish and trout nipping at them, larger offerings lasted longer. Some customers were leery about casting such heavy terminal gear, so the guides often did the honours. Once the sinker stopped moving in the current, the rod was placed in its holder, then the reel drag was adjusted until it was just snug enough to prevent the current from pulling off line.

Some of the sturgeon pools covered several acres. There, bottom-feeding fish cruised the murky depths using their highly developed sense of smell to locate food. This was where the waiting came in.

Folding chairs were included with the equipment, as were huge box lunches, large vacuum jugs of coffee, and plenty of cold drinks. Anglers whiled away their time exploring the shoreline for jade, reading, playing cards, or simply dozing in the sun. Bites took anywhere from minutes to hours (I once hooked a frisky five-footer within 15 seconds of my bait hitting the water). If no fish had investigated at least one of our baits within an hour, everything was reloaded and we departed for a new location.

Despite those express-train hits experienced by Mike Wells and Chuck Cronmiller, the bite of a sturgeon is usually deceptively gentle — more like a small fish toying with the bait. When a bite is detected, the rod is quickly removed from its holder — but the waiting game continues. A sliding sinker permits a fish to move around without feeling undue resistance, so the angler waits until the slack is taken up before setting the hook.

If a fish is hooked, what follows always surprises first-time sturgeon anglers. Perhaps because sturgeon look so much like huge suckers, it is assumed they are slow, sluggish fighters. Wrong. "It's the jumps that amaze people," said Bryan. "We hooked one in '84 that would have gone at least 14 feet long. When a fish that big decides to run, all you can do is jump in the boat and follow it. That's what we were doing when it decided to jump. It came straight up out of the water — right beside us — just like one of those submarine-launched missiles, then toppled over, fortunately away from the boat. I'll tell you, Jonesy, when you've got that much fish hanging right over top of you, you kind of get religion in a hurry." He grinned, shaking his head. "I was really quite relieved when that one got away."

Clarence told me that their customers hooked a few monsters each season, and the best fish they had ever landed was a 10-foot, 542-pounder. He guesstimated Bryan's lost 14-footer would have topped 1,000 pounds.

Our two-day venture ended with 11 sturgeon beached. Frank Gavin landed a 52-incher, and a high-jumping 40-incher gave me some exciting moments before being tagged and released. Fortunately, Chuck's nine fish were all shy of the 39-inch minimum size limit. Talk about a blessing. Two days of listening to constant reminders of his fishing prowess was bad enough; a legal-sized fish would have made it totally unbearable.

APPEARANCES

Below me, a faded red canoe drifted slowly off the bay's rocky shoreline, its lone occupant wielding his fly rod with practised skill and grace. Ralph lives and works shifts in the city, but spends weekends and holidays at his cabin on the shore of the bay. No one knows the lake as well as Ralph, so I readied my camera. The afternoon light was good, and it probably wouldn't take long before I got some action shots of him fighting a fish. The only problem was that Ralph is a confirmed bachelor who dresses like a tramp at his cabin, and never shaves.

I perched on a suitable rock while waiting, observing how methodically he prospected each potential location. A few minutes had passed when I detected a faint droning sound. Airplane?... No — an outboard motor, obviously high-powered. Unusual on this small lake. It grew louder, then a wide-bodied boat appeared from around the point. Behind, a water skier was doing an admirable job of maintaining his balance while crisscrossing back and forth, jumping over the wake.

When the boat curved gracefully toward Ralph's canoe on what appeared to be a collision course, I worried that the driver might not see him, but it finally veered sharply away. As they roared past, much too close for comfort, the driver and two occupants shouted, simultaneously raising cans of beer in salute. The skier, leaning almost parallel to the water, swung wide, skittering within 20 feet of the canoe as the lacy curtain of water from his skis arced high into the air, totally drenching Ralph. Moments later the boat's wake arrived, almost capsizing him.

As boat and skier faded into the distance, Ralph reeled in his line, laid his rod in the canoe, then picked up his paddle and headed toward the cabin. While watching, I recalled an old joke: if you are fishing and a water skier starts harassing you, give him a cold can of beer — but don't forget to lead him by about 15 feet.

I walked back to my van and drove down the road to the turn-off to Ralph's cabin. By the time I arrived he had changed into dry clothes, and was buttoning his shirt.

"Hope you dried behind your ears," I said by way of greeting.

"Yep. I saw you up on the bluff. Spying on me, eh?"

"Nope — taking photographs."

"That right?" Ralph did up the last button. "And what did you photograph?"

"A motor-drive sequence. Ten shots of them buzzing your canoe, and the water skier giving you a bath — which they probably thought you really needed."

"Very funny." Ralph scratched the greying stubble on his chin, then picked up his electric shaver. "Which lens were you using?"

"Two hundred."

"Hmm ... strong enough to read the registration number?"

I nodded. "Even the brand of beer they were drinking."

For the first time since my arrival, Ralph smiled. "Any chance of seeing them when you get the film developed?"

"No problem."

The shaver squealed and rattled like a vacuum cleaner sucking up broken glass, defeating further attempts at conversation. When he finished, Ralph explained that he was off to the city to start a string of evening shifts, but first he planned on stopping by the resort — which has the lake's only boat-launching ramp.

After locking the cabin, we said our goodbyes and strolled to our vehicles. Ralph waved casually and drove off, but I just sat there for a while, musing over the difference a shave and the sharply-pressed police sergeant's uniform makes in my friend's appearance.

LURKING LAKERS

As Gary Hill and I neared the end of our telephone conversation he asked, "By the way, how's old Cronmiller doing?"

"Chuck's doing great," I replied. "For a guy who's supposed to be retired, he's really keeping busy these days. He invented a new electronic device a few months ago, and just took out a patent on it. We think he'll make a bundle on it."

"Hey, that's great! What is it?"

"It's a miniature, hypersensitive detector that you attach to the tip of your fishing rod so you can tell whether or not you're fighting a lake trout."

"Argh! You got me again, you bugger!"

It all started during the winter of 1991, when Gary telephoned to brag about the fishing he had enjoyed after moving a year earlier to Atlin, in the northwestern corner of British Columbia. "Atlin Lake has probably got the best population of lakers in Canada," he said. "Lots of small fish under 10 pounds, but some real wall-hangers in the 20- to 40-pound range. Okay, stop yawning! We've got big grayling, too — some over 20 inches — and pike to 30 pounds plus. Get your butt up here and give 'em a try."

Gary and I go back to the late 1970s, when I was an air weapons instructor at Camp Borden, Ontario, and he operated a thriving taxidermy business near Orillia. One of the top lake trout and muskie anglers in Southern Ontario, Gary started leading fishing tours to the Yukon in 1977. He first visited Atlin in 1982, then relocated there in the spring of 1990.

It is no secret that lake trout are absolute rock bottom on my list of exciting fish to catch, but those grayling and pike numbers sounded too good to pass up. When I suggested a trip north to Chuck Cronmiller, he agreed, so we started making plans.

* * * *

On July 30, Gary Hill and Bobbie Whelan met us at the Whitehorse airport. After loading our equipment into his pickup truck we headed 40 miles southeast on the Alaska Highway toward Jake's Corner, where we swung south toward Atlin on Highway 7, a 60-mile stretch of moderately smooth gravel road. While en route, our hosts explained that Atlin had been a thriving gold-rush town of 5,000 at the turn of the century, but the permanent population now hovered around 500, with a similar number of summer residents who fled south for the long winters.

Bobbie, a long-time Atlin resident, said that while the area's spectacular scenery attracted scores of tourists annually, relatively few anglers realized that the region offers some of the finest fishing opportunities left on this continent. Atlin Lake is 85 miles long and averages about two to five miles wide, making it the largest natural body of freshwater in B.C. In addition, several other road-accessible lakes have excellent fishing, and there are a multitude of seldom-fished, fly-in locations that yield everything from pike and lake trout to sea-run chinook, coho and steelhead.

The following morning Gary had to crate a black bear mount for shipment, so Bobbie took us on a driving tour of the area — assuring us that the chilly wind and icy rain were unseasonable and wouldn't last. After touring the pioneer town we drove south to the Llewellyn Glacier viewpoint, overlooking one of the largest ice fields in North America. Our next stop was Warm Springs, a small, shallow pool heated by underground thermal springs. A mile and a half beyond was "The Grotto," where a crystal stream gushed from a small cave to flow over a luxurious bed of watercress. I still recall it as one of the prettiest spots I have ever seen.

When we returned, Gary was in the yard checking over his 16-foot aluminum boat. I walked over and snarled in my best Humphrey Bogart imitation, "Hill, let's get one thing straight: I know you're going to drag us out to fish for lake trout, and I'll go with you — once. If you try any more than once, I'll hitch-hike back to Whitehorse. Okay?"

"Jones, you wouldn't know a good fish if you caught one. Anyway, you won't have to worry about lake trout at all if this damned wind doesn't let up."

It didn't that day or the next, so we fished for grayling at Surprise Lake, and pike at Palmer Lake. The results were dismal: two 12-inch grayling and a dozen or so pike, none over two pounds. Some trophies. By the end of day two, snide remarks about our friend's questionable guiding ability had reached terminal velocity, and Gary's life was not worth living.

"Get even" time arrived on the third morning, Gary having decided the wind was down enough to punish me with some lake trout fishing. After launching at the public ramp in town, we headed about three miles across Atlin Lake toward a cluster of small islands off the western shore. Low clouds made for a grey, dreary day, and despite the fact that it was August 2, we could see our breath in the air. Between the stiff breeze and choppy water, it was a cold, lumpy, uncomfortable crossing.

Gary had small downriggers mounted on each side of his boat. He quickly rigged a large, gold-coloured Williams Flasher spoon to the left-hand outfit, then lowered the cannon ball to 70 feet. On the right went an equally large red-and-yellow Husky Devle, which he lowered to 80 feet. The lures had been down scarcely five minutes when Gary suddenly barked, "There!" and dove for the left-hand rod. Pulling it from the holder he leaned forward and tried handing it to me. "Here!"

"No!" I recoiled in mock horror, ramming my hands deeper into my coat pockets.

"Take it!"

"No! Give it to Chuck — he's never caught one before."

Gary swung the rod over to Chuck, who grabbed it with both hands, then announced, "It got off."

"No it didn't!" Gary yelped. "Reel it in!"

"But there's nothing there," Chuck explained, rather patiently, I thought.

"Yes there is! Reel it in!"

Chuck shrugged and started reeling. I still recall the look on his face when a comatose, six-pound lake trout appeared on the surface. It was the first of five beautifully-marked lakers brought to the boat over the next hour. They ranged in size from four to 14 pounds, and all fought with the vim and vigour usually associated with sea cucumbers. In the meantime, the wind had been increasing, and the waves were starting to whitecap. I had been photographing all of the thrilling "action," and was shivering so hard my teeth were clacking like castanets when Gary suggested we head home. The trip back was colder and rougher, with the added attraction of wet spray billowing over the bow. Fortunately, as I was on the bow seat my body protected Gary and Chuck from most of the spray.

Later, back in our guest cabin, Chuck sipped a scotch while I got into dry clothes. Despite all of the heart-stopping action he had experienced in such a short time, he appeared rather glum.

"Something wrong?" I asked.

Chuck cleared his throat, then said in an accusing manner, "Is there something you're not telling me?"

"About?"

"Today."

"What about it?"

"I feel like I'm participating in a 'snipe hunt,' but you're not letting me in on the joke."

"Joke?" Then it dawned on me. "Charles — am I led to believe you're a little underwhelmed with the fighting abilities of those lake trout?"

"What fight?" he demanded hotly.

"Well, I distinctly remember seeing a fin flicker on one of them — but that was after it came out of the water, so it might have been the wind blowing it."

Chuck shook his head in disbelief. "I've had more trouble reeling in kelp. Don't they ever fight any harder than that?"

"People keep telling me they do, but I've yet to see it. I've caught 'em in Quebec, Ontario, Saskatchewan; I've caught 'em through the ice on handlines and on the surface with ultralight spinning gear, but I've yet to have one put up anything remotely resembling a decent scrap."

"So why do people fish for them?"

"Beats me. Lots of people are absolutely nuts about them. Look at Gary: he's caught salmon, steelhead, muskie, bass — you name it — but he's still a 100%, gold-plated lake trout fanatic."

Nor is he alone. Whatever the attraction, tens of thousands of other North American anglers also hold lake trout in high regard. While it's true I love twisting the tails of aficionados like Gary, I try to keep an open mind. It's just that so far, catching lake trout has been like voting for politicians: I always end up disappointed.

After supper that evening, we retired to the living room. It took all of eight or 10 seconds for the conversation to get around to fish, whereupon Gary commented that lake trout were actually char, not a trout. I promptly disagreed. "That was then and this is now," I explained. "A few years ago, interior Dolly Varden were reclassified as 'bull trout,' and their Latin name was changed from *Salvelinus malma* to *Salvelinus confluentus.*" (Surprisingly, Gary didn't seem overly impressed with my ability to speak in italics.)

"More recently," I continued, "ichthyologists decided rainbow trout were actually members of the Pacific salmon family, so they reclassified them and changed their Latin name *Salmo gairdneri* to *Oncorhynchus mykiss.* Now they have decided lake trout were misclassified as char, so their Latin name was changed from *Salvelinus namaycush* to *Giganticus pacificus sluggus.*"

Gary's bushy black eyebrows knotted briefly into a puzzled frown, then he shook his head, "Yeah, yeah — Giant Pacific slug." He raised a truly massive fist and shook it menacingly in my direction. "One of these days, Jones...."

* * * *

Our trip to Atlin actually ended well. Once the weather warmed and the wind let up, Surprise Lake and the Pine River yielded some dandy grayling to three pounds. At Kuthai Lake, a small, fly-in lake on the Pacific drainage, we encountered some fine, high-jumping pike to 12 pounds, and Chuck lost what appeared to be at least a 10-pound steelhead. He then landed and released a buck sockeye of eight pounds or so. Quite a day. However, the best part of the whole trip was that Gary honoured his promise and didn't take us lake trout fishing again.

FISHING ON SELF-DESTRUCT

The first time Hotchkiss visited Vancouver Island, he brought his medium-action spinning outfit, the one he used for smallmouth bass and walleye in the rivers and lakes around Ottawa. "Don't imagine it's any good for those giant salmon you're always bragging about," he said.

"Matter of fact, Hotch, it's fine for what we'll be doing tomorrow." It was mid-September and there was good coho action off Comox. "What have you got on that coffee grinder for line?"

"Two hundred yards of 12-pound test."

"That'll do in a pinch — we can always try chasing the big ones."

His eyebrows arched slightly. "Two hundred yards isn't enough?"

"Sometimes 400 yards isn't enough."

"Hah! I'll believe that when I see it."

The next day, as our boat drifted offshore from Cape Lazo, I showed Hotch how to rig a Buzz Bomb by threading his line through the metal body, then installed a tiny rubber bumper before tying on a treble hook. He grumbled that the "Bug Bomb" looked like a hook sharpener.

"Buzz Bomb," I corrected. "It represents a crippled baitfish."

"You must have some weird-lookin' baitfish out here." His eyes narrowed. "Say, you gonna use one too?" I nodded and withdrew an identical lure from my tackle box.

When salmon slash through a school of herring, several baitfish are stunned or killed, then they sink downward, usually with a rolling or spiralling action that Buzz Bombs imitate perfectly. Salmon cruising below see what looks like an easy meal and pick it off.

I gave Hotch a quick demonstration on how to control the lure's descent by using his fingertip to feather the line as it rotated around the spool flange, then how to jig it with a slow, two-foot lift, followed by a fast drop that caused the lure to go horizontal and rotate downward.

We started out catching bottom fish: two four-pound quillback rockfish, a small copper rockfish, a feisty little lingcod, and two 30-inch-long dogfish. A slow day by West Coast standards, but Hotch was intrigued by the strange, new fish.

When I finally spotted seagulls hovering and diving at the water, we cranked in our lures and raced toward the action. As we drew near, flashes of sunlight reflected brilliantly from the silver sides of virtually millions of frantically leaping herring. "Cast right along the edge and let your jig flutter down beside them."

Hotch did as instructed, then, feeling a bump on his line, hauled back on the rod and promptly foul-hooked a coho somewhere near its tail. It leaped right beside the boat, a pewter-coloured, hook-nosed male in the mid to high teens. Its back half out of the water, it streaked away, a white plume of water roostertailing behind. Impressive.

At about 200 feet, Hotch's reel started squealing — a thin, reedy sound that built in volume as the amount of line decreased in direct proportion to the rapidly departing fish's distance, which in turn increased the spool's speed of rotation. Somewhere between 300 and 400 feet, a wisp of smoke curled up from Hotch's reel, then his line parted at or near the hook. I quit pulling on the starter cord.

Several seconds passed. "Hotch, if you don't blink, your eyeballs are gonna dry out."

His voice weak and quavering with emotion, Hotch began a long, rambling, expletive-filled soliloquy about recent events, eventually concluding that it was physically impossible for any fish to swim so far, so fast.

Hotchkiss eventually recovered enough to boat three prime coho ranging from seven to nine pounds. After which he begrudgingly admitted Bug Bombs were good lures after all — even if they did look like hook sharpeners.

AN ANCIENT ART

If the term "fly-tying" conjures visions of some strange approach to insect control, it's time you were introduced to one of the most interesting and enjoyable pastimes associated with recreational angling. Creating fishing lures from bits of feather and hair is an art that is easily learned, yet one that never seems to lose its attraction. I have friends in their eighties who sit down before a fly-tying vise with as much enthusiasm today as I am sure they displayed 50 or 60 years ago.

Despite the term, the finished products leaving a tier's vise seldom look like flying insects. More often they bear a striking resemblance to silver-sided minnows, crustaceans, the nymphal or pupal stages of aquatic insects, or terrestrial insects like beetles, crickets and grasshoppers. To further confuse the issue, another group of "flies" imitates creatures like earthworms, frogs, snakes, mice and baby muskrats. Collectively, this entire hodgepodge of fakes is called "imitators," meaning they are relatively faithful representations of creatures found in the food chain of various fish species.

A second fly category, referred to as "attractors," resembles nothing that flies, swims, walks, or crawls on its belly like a reptile.

One of the most famous patterns in this group is the Parmachene Belle, a red-and-white concoction tied to resemble a dismembered brook-trout fin. Not the sort of thing one normally finds swimming about on its own, but the pattern can be quite productive at times, particularly for brook trout, bull trout, Dolly Varden and cutthroats. Whether fish strike these gaudy creations out of curiosity, anger, fear or hunger is a question that will probably never be answered satisfactorily — but at times attractors catch fish when even the most realistic imitators are snubbed.

Many anglers claim that the only thing more thrilling than catching your first fish on a fly, is catching your first fish on a fly you have tied yourself. Over the years, several friends have admitted they started fly-tying out of curiosity; however, once that first fish fell for one of their creations, their casual pastime became a joyful obsession.

The person generally credited with initiating this intriguing hobby was a Macedonian fellow with the tongue-twisting name of Ichthuoulkos. As the story goes, he conceived the idea for his first artificial fly while watching what were probably brown trout or European grayling feeding on insects floating on the surface of the Astraeus River. When he saw fish occasionally rising to take floating duck feathers, he concluded they probably bore some similarity to an insect. This sounds quite plausible, for even today it's fairly common to see fish rise to small feathers floating freely on the water. This is purely supposition, of course, for Ichthuoulkos lived around 200 BC.

That he knew a good thing when he saw it is borne out by the fact that some 400 years later, a Roman scribe named Claudius Aelianus wrote in *Natura Animalium* of Macedonian anglers fishing with "flies." His record stated, "They fasten red wool around a hook and fix to the wool two feathers that grow under a cock's wattles and which in colour are like wax." He was, no doubt, referring to the red wax commonly used for official seals on documents.

Centuries later, in *The Boke of St. Albans*, printed in 1496, Dame Juliana Berners recommended using a fly having "... a body of roddy wull and lappid abowte wyth blacke silke; the wynges of the drake of redde capons hakyll."

That original Macedonian pattern still has several offspring which enjoy popularity with anglers, among them the Red Ibis and Red Dragon. Obviously, you can't argue with success.

* * * *

That fly-tiers are inventive and artistic is well-illustrated by the jewel-like beauty of traditional Atlantic salmon flies. The majority of the most famous patterns evolved during the late 1800s and early 1900s. Tiers then displayed great imagination and ability with regard to the intricacies of their designs, plus an obvious flair for sound business practices. During that period, exotic fowl enjoyed a great deal of popularity throughout much of Britain, and it did not take the canny tiers long to discover that flies dressed with gaily-coloured plumage commanded higher prices than those fashioned from mundane barnyard fowl feathers.

With gaudy golden and silver pheasants, toucans, parrots and peacocks at their disposal, fly patterns created by the tiers became more intricate and involved as they tried to outdo their competitors. It was from this era that still-famous patterns like the Dusty Miller, Durham Ranger and Jock Scott emerged. The latter provides a good indication of the lengths to which tiers went, for the original Jock Scott incorporated 23 different types of material in its construction.

Early North American salmon anglers did not have experienced tiers on hand to create flies for them, so they turned to tying their own. As they were a little short of ornamental fowl during those early days, they had to make do with whatever was on hand. The resulting patterns were often drab in comparison with their British counterparts, but much easier to tie. They also proved a worthy match for fancy flies at catching fish. Collectively, the output from this simplified form of fly construction became known as "Canadian Guide Patterns."

While the names of British flies were almost as pretty as their patterns — Silver Abbey, Lady Caroline, Blue Charm — those evolving from North American shores have often displayed a touch of ribald humour. A few of my favourites are Zug Bug, Humboldt Railbird, Strawberry Blond, Woolly Bugger and Norwegian Moustache.

Fly-tying as a hobby is gaining in popularity in a roundabout way. Urban residents often turn to the out-of-doors to escape pressures of the daily rat race, and many end up with fishing rods in their hands for the first time since they were kids — some for the first time in their lives. As their interest and expertise increase and improve, many broaden their horizons by making the transition from spinning or casting tackle to the more personally challenging sport of fly-fishing. Once this conversion starts, it is only a matter of time before thoughts of tying their own flies begin to germinate. Unfortunately, a large percentage never get beyond the thinking stage. Some are frightened off by self-proclaimed "experts" who love to expound on how difficult and demanding the task is. Ignore them. Life is far too full of blowhards. If you have the manual dexterity to tie your shoe laces without tangling up your fingers too badly, you can master the basics of tying flies.

Other would-be tiers shy away from getting involved because they think it will wreak havoc with their bank account. Wrong. If you shop around with a bit of prudence, it's possible to start with a fairly decent selection of equipment and material for about the same price as a bottle of premium, single malt scotch — and tying flies won't give you a hangover.

If you have friends who tie flies, butter them up for a few lessons and some advice on selecting the necessary paraphernalia to make a modest start. Other options are organized courses which are often offered at night schools or community colleges. There are numerous entry-level books available to guide neophyte tiers through everything from the initial purchase of equipment and material to the techniques of tying a few basic patterns. Once you feel comfortable with these, there are virtually thousands of books that detail advanced tying techniques and myriad patterns.

Like many endeavours, tying flies is a matter of learning basic techniques, then practising them until they are mastered. Novices usually start cautiously, then, when they feel more comfortable about wielding bobbins, scissors and hackle pliers, they progress to more involved patterns. A good example is starting with relatively simple streamer patterns before tackling winged dry flies. However, the fun really starts when tradition is thrown to the wind and tiers start experimenting with their own creations. It is from these exploratory pursuits that new patterns evolve, some of them very innovative and productive. Whether you remain a duffer or move up to the level of world-famous tiers like Poul Jorgensen, Jack Shaw, Torill Kolbu, or Dave Whitlock, there are few more pleasant ways to while away time — or unwind after a hard day — than indulging in the ancient art of tying flies.

WINTER FUN

Vera, my prairie belle, is a marvellous cook, keeps our home in good order without being fanatical, enjoys mowing lawns and digging gardens, and absolutely refuses to let me wash or dry dishes. However, my jewel is flawed. She hails from Manitoba; thus, she is not only used to cold winter weather, but actually enjoys it. I, on the other hand, originated on the West Coast, where harsh winters were coped with by sleeping in late until the frost melted.

Winter has always rated low on my popularity scale, right down there with blackflies, mosquitoes, warm beer and plugged toilets. It is best spent reading, tying flies, tinkering with fishing tackle, or hibernating — all near a constant source of heat. I find it curious that so many people lack the mental strength necessary to ward off "winter hysteria," an insidious malady resulting from the mind-altering vapours released by freshly-fallen snow. This, of course, explains those hordes of people, young and old, who intentionally venture out into the stuff for endless hours of what they call "winter activities."

I have always been recognized as a fairly patient, reasonable person, but I do have limits. You can, therefore, appreciate my shock when Vera once suggested we take up cross-country skiing. This was during one of the Ontario stages of my military career, when I considered it punishment enough to have friends who continued the cruel myth that ice fishing is fun. Now my own mate stood before me, proposing such a revolting indecency that my mind reeled with horror. "Just think," she enthused, "we can even use the skis to go out on Lake Simcoe and Couchiching when we go ice fishing."

When I finally calmed down, my response was rational, emphatic, and, of course, totally negative. I explained firmly that there are some things I simply will not do, under any circumstances — even for her.

* * * *

The sole of a cross-country ski boot protrudes at the toe and has indentations to accept three steel pins of the binding, which are anchored to the ski. This forms a unique hinge system that allows skiers to pitch forward onto their faces, using friction to slow otherwise fatal plunges down sheer precipices. Falling to either side also enables the ski tips to hinge back and make sharp contact with the head, thus expelling compacted snow from various sensory orifices, usually with explosive force. Pin bindings do not hinge to the rear, however, so falling backwards often results in minor problems like sprains, torn ligaments, fractures or hernias.

Steering is physically impossible on cross-country skis. The way one is aimed at the lip of a near-vertical slope — the only type of hill encountered — is the direction one continues travelling, unless, of course, one is deflected off a solid, immovable object. Photographs and films of cross-country skiers doing graceful banks and telemark turns are simply part of the sham perpetrated by the ski industry. What they do not show are the slender steel wires which connect those skiers to helium-filled balloons high overhead.

As evasive tactics are impossible, the ability to arrest forward motion should be considered simply a preventive measure useful for sustaining life. Stopping is accomplished by falling down. This tactic should always be given serious consideration while one is hurtling out of control toward rock outcroppings, large trees, stationary vehicles, or rustic log cabins. I quickly mastered four basic manoeuvres: the somersaulting ricochet; forward noseplow; horizontal whirling dervish; and the screaming cartwheel. I was, in fact, considered an expert on these subjects, and became living proof of the wonders of modern medicine.

The only thing more disagreeable than cross-country skiing was cross-country skiing combined with ice fishing, especially when friends like Merton or Hotchkiss wanted to target lake trout. One evening, while I was earnestly trying to talk her out of another planned torture session the following day, Vera said, "Can you tell me one other pastime where you can have that much fun with your clothes on, and meet so many interesting people?"

After giving her question some serious thought, I decided that the only pastime worthy of consideration was armed combat, and the interesting people included first aid attendants, ambulance drivers, nursing staff, doctors, physiotherapists, and chiropractors. It didn't matter — we went anyway.

TYING FLIES

My plateau of fly-tying competence was established quite early in life, and I have maintained it only through constant practice. This has meant spending long stints at the fly-tying vise when I would rather be doing yard work, house repairs, or similar interesting and fulfilling pastimes, but such are the demands of artistic endeavour.

Aside from occasional warnings by Vera that I should be careful of "The Heap," she shows little interest in my efforts. That's what she calls the old desk down in our basement, where I create my feathered jewels. She honestly believes it is a living organism with bad breath and an insatiable appetite for inanimate objects, and that it might someday turn on me if I am not careful. I have tried reasoning with her, but to no avail — she claims to have heard it growling at her, and now refuses to go near that corner of the room.

True, a slight aroma emanates from The Heap, but it's probably nothing more than one of the beautiful hides salvaged from various road-kills last summer. I suspect it might be the Norway rat skin, but can't seem to locate it, even though I distinctly recall placing it on the desk. Like many other objects and tools, it seems to have disappeared, almost as though it was absorbed into the multi-coloured mound sprawling over the desk top.

I was about eight when I started tying flies. My early creations had lumpy bodies, odd-sized wings that jutted drunkenly from one side or the other, and hackle collars that found ways to unravel

mysteriously through the heavy cotton sewing thread that formed
their huge, globe-shaped heads. They were tied on black japanned
hooks, No. 1 and 2 Siwash models with long, thick points that were
dull as four-inch nails, and ringed eyes I could almost stick my little
finger through.

Ugly as they were, when dangled from the tip of my old tele-
scoping, tubular-steel rod they occasionally caught fish. It's possible
those little trout struck out of fear or revulsion rather than hunger
— or they might well have been mentally deficient. Whichever, they
were as juicy and tasty as fish caught on worms or grasshoppers.

Recently, while I was at the kitchen table having a mid-afternoon
coffee, Vera came in with an envelope she had discovered while
rummaging through an old trunk filled with family photographs and
trinkets. It contained one of my earliest attempts at tying flies. I
smiled. Mother was always saving locks of hair and pressing flowers
in books. She had probably secreted the fly away as a keepsake,
where it remained undetected for nearly five decades. But then
again, she might have been hiding it out of sheer embarrassment.

The newly-found fly's tail was a cluster of fibres from a shocking
pink feather, probably filched from one of Mother's Sunday go-to-
church hats. Tied in halfway down the bend of the No. 1 Siwash
hook, it drooped at a right angle to the shank. The body — thick as
a pencil — was of bright yellow wool, with a single strand of red
wool spiralling unevenly from back to front. A clump of dark tan hair
that I recognized as being snipped from the tail of Drooler, our long-
suffering dog, formed a wing that curled off on a distinct tangent to
the left. Its bulky head, which has become my trademark, was
daubed with aluminum paint. Without doubt, it was a world-class,
monumentally ugly fly.

A few minutes later, Crony stopped by to visit. While I was
pouring his coffee, he spotted my fly lying on the table. He picked it
up and studied it closely for several seconds before nodding approv-
ingly. "Not bad. I always thought that with more practice you'd
improve — and here's the proof."

§FIVE
MORE ONTARIO MEMORIES

STARTING THE SEASON

"Good afternoon, sir. Would you mind telling me what you're fishing for?"

I glanced around and saw that my inquisitor was a tall, rugged-looking Ontario conservation officer.

"Well," I replied, "pike, muskie, walleye and bass are all closed, and the crappie haven't shown up on their spawning run, so I guess I'm fishing for perch and sunfish."

I finished cranking my lure in and lifted it from the frigid waters of the Rideau River for his inspection. I was using a five-foot-long ultralight spinning rod, and a tiny reel filled with four-pound-test-line. He studied the No. 0, silver Mepps spinner dangling from an eight-inch strand of woven steel.

"If you're after sunfish and perch, why the steel leader?" he asked.

"Because I know pike are closed, and you know pike are closed, but the pike don't know they're closed. And I don't like donating a lure every time one of them takes a smack at it."

He threw back his head and laughed. "Yeah, I see your point. I guess that light line wouldn't stand much of a chance." He touched his forefinger to his cap brim in casual salute. "Well, good luck and don't catch 'em all."

As he walked back over the uneven ground toward his car, I resumed casting. It was a bright, sunlit day, but winter's chill was still in the air, and chunks of ice nestled in shaded portions along the shoreline. It was probably too early, but it had been a long winter and I had a restless urge to hold the smooth cork handle of a fishing rod in my hand.

Easter weekend is normally a time to count on the black crappie run, but as ice still coated the river, the water was too cold to trigger their spawning urge. When the discomfort of numbed fingers and ears finally outweighed the enjoyment of fishing, I reluctantly trudged back to the car and made my way home. I hadn't received so much as a tentative nibble for my exertion, but felt satisfied, nevertheless.

* * * *

Two days later, I returned with Jose Mello and Larry Bourgeois. We all had basically the same types of ultralight spinning outfits, and our tackle boxes bulged with minuscule offerings.

"You going to throw the 'Tin Goose' in or fish from shore?" Larry asked as he threaded line through his rod guides.

"Guess we might as well fish from shore until we see what's what," I replied.

We were at the point where a large slough drains into the Rideau River near Kars, about 12 miles upstream from Ottawa. The large, shallow expanse of water is home to many species of waterfowl, turtles, frogs, raccoons, and other assorted shoreline dwellers. It is also an excellent breeding area for pike, muskie and crappie.

We walked onto the bridge spanning the channel and peered into the water. The weak-tea tinge peculiar to the Rideau system made it difficult to see fish, even with the aid of polarized glasses. Larry pointed toward a light-coloured patch of gravel on the bottom. "See over there? Looks like a bunch of small perch."

"Well," I said, "if the perch are around, there might be a few sunnies and bluegills. Let's give 'er a try."

My companions opted to fish the channel's upstream side, so I headed down the opposite bank. I started with a grey-bodied No. 0 Rooster Tail, but nothing was tempted by my hackle-tailed offering. I worked slowly down the shoreline toward the main river, alternating the depth and speed of my retrieves, seeking the right combination.

Shortly after I switched to a yellow Rooster Tail of the same size, my persistence was rewarded by the sharp tug of a fish hitting the lure. A spectacular battle raged for nearly five seconds, then I hoisted a lunker, four-inch pumpkinseed into the air. Grinning like an idiot, I held the cocky little sunfish in the palm of my hand for a moment, admiring the colourful tapestry of its saucer-shaped body. The tiny, barbless hook came easily from its lip, then I lowered it back into the water.

When a few more casts produced nothing but a two-foot length of water-logged branch, I ambled over to the car and untied my 14-foot Sportspal from the roof rack. My companions had disappeared around the bend, so I slid the canoe partially into the water, then located two basketball-sized boulders to place in its bow for ballast. As I nosed the wide-beamed craft into the main channel, I spotted my friends about 50 yards upstream. Something didn't look right. Larry was leaning forward, hands on his knees, staring intently into the water, and Jose's rod was bent double. I assumed he had snagged bottom until I saw the slender shaft of fibreglass start pulsating from the antics of an unseen fish. Jose grimaced at the pressure being exerted on his tackle.

"Somebody bite off more than he could chew?" I called out.

"He's got a bloody muskie on!" Larry answered. "Looks like it'll go eight or 10 pounds."

The fish chose this moment to rise to the surface and thrash about rather sluggishly. Obviously, the fight was nearing its end. Although it was the first time Jose had ever used an ultralight outfit, he played the fish like a seasoned pro on that gossamer strand of four-pound-test monofilament.

The weary fish was finally drawn close enough to Larry's outstretched hand for him to grasp it firmly over the gill covers. A twist with his needle-nose pliers removed the hook of the tiny No. 0 Mepps from the muskie's tooth-studded jaws, then he briefly held it up for admiring or envious glances — depending on who did the looking.

"Now I see why you use a steel leader," said Jose, as Larry eased the fish back into the water and administered a bit of artificial respiration to help speed it on its way. With shaking hands, Jose attempted to light a cigarette, causing much mirth in the peanut gallery. Landing one's first muskie on regulation tackle is enough to cause some active twitching and quivering, but Jose's accomplishment with ultralight tackle had his hands vibrating as though he was hanging onto a jackhammer.

"How have you guys been making out — besides that pathetic little hammer handle?" I asked.

While Jose looked around for something hard or unsanitary — preferably both — to throw at me, Larry said they had caught and released several small perch and sunfish, all on silver Mepps. "That muskie was probably cruising around, planning to make a meal of some of the ones we were catching. Then Jose dunked his lure in the right place at the right time."

Neither of my friends was interested in joining me in the canoe, so I paddled downstream to the channel mouth and resumed casting my Rooster Tail. I was contemplating a lure change when a sudden jolt announced something on the business end of my rigging. What followed puzzled me, for the fish didn't feel very large, but its struggles were aggressively strong. The mystery was solved when a beady-eyed, bewhiskered head popped through the surface, and I hoisted a 10-inch bullhead into the canoe.

Bullheads don't have much going for them in the beauty department. What can be said about a fish cloaked in mottled, muddy-brown, with a dingy, yellow belly; eyes that look like two black map tacks; and thick, rubbery lips sporting tendril-like barbels? However, despite their homely appearance, they are favoured by legions of anglers who know beneath that humble-looking hide is some delicious eating.

What really surprised me was that it hit so close to the surface, for bullheads are bottom dwellers and feeders. The fighting abilities of these pugnacious little fish never cease to amaze me, for they often outfight many highly-touted game fish, especially when taken on light gear. Twisting the hook free and allowing it to drop back into the water, I told the chisel-headed little scrapper, "Go home and breed a new race of surface-feeders."

And so our afternoon wore on: enjoyable, but hardly fast-paced — except for Jose's muskie. A few more pumpkinseeds and perch were hoisted over the side of my canoe and released, as was a spunky, hand-sized bluegill. My companions fared a bit better, having discovered an apparent "hot spot." Although their mixed bag was on the small side, the fish were plentiful.

I beached my canoe and was strolling toward the car, intent on raiding my thermos for coffee, when a car eased onto the gravelled shoulder. It was the friendly C.O. I had met on my previous trip. "Hello again," he said. "Any luck?"

As I detailed the afternoon's events, he was amused that a muskie hit such a tiny lure, and as amazed as I that a bullhead had attacked my lure on the surface. "But still no crappie," I complained. "I guess the water hasn't warmed up enough."

"Crappie? Hell, if you want crappie, you should be fishing up at Burritts Rapids — the water's crawling with them."

I glanced at my watch. There was about two and a half hours of daylight left, so I thanked the C.O. and jogged across the field to give my companions the news. After a flurry of activity, our gear was stowed, the canoe lashed back onto the roof rack, and we were on the road for Burritts Rapids, 15 miles upstream.

After pulling into the parking lot located above the canal locks, we grabbed our tackle and headed down the steep, lawn-covered slopes below the locks. The C.O. had not exaggerated — the short length of canal separating the lock gate from the river's main body was swarming with crappie.

"This is more like it!" Larry exclaimed as he cast into the teeming mass of fish.

Two other anglers were in the area — a man about 30, and his son, maybe seven or eight. Neither was having any success because their lures were much too large, better suited for bass than crappie. We started with No. 0 Mepps spinners, but quickly discovered that while the fish would follow, they wouldn't strike. Larry suggested we try tiny, $1/32$-ounce jigs with soft plastic grub-shaped bodies. Instant success. We would toss out a minuscule lure, then let it settle slowly toward bottom at its own speed. The journey seldom lasted long before it was inhaled by a slab-sided "papermouth."

The young father quickly noted our good fortune, then delved into his tackle box for two white-bodied jigs with fluorescent-red heads. They were about twice the size of ours, but the crappie were co-operative. Within a matter of minutes, the father and son had a respectable number of fish on the grass-covered bank. The action continued fast and furious, then the sun's departure caused a noticeable drop in temperature, reminding us we were not too long out of winter's clutches.

We had probably caught over 100 fish between us, but only two dozen of the largest were in the trunk of my car when we headed home. We had agreed beforehand to keep only enough for a late-evening fish fry, leaving the next day free for an early start to return to the locks and stock up our respective freezers. Our reasoning was simple: it takes far longer to clean and prepare crappies for long-term storage than it does to catch them.

That night, as I lay in bed with a bellyful of succulent, deep-fried crappie, I mused about the throngs of anglers waiting impatiently for the pike and walleye season to open. I decided that if people ever realized the abundance of fish available to ultralight spinning enthusiasts between ice-out and the game fish opening, a lot of happy tackle-shop owners might be hard pressed to keep a supply of the slender little fairy-wands and midget reels in stock.

JUMPING THE GUN

When the old wooden bridge was torn down, it was replaced by a modern structure of concrete and steel. Extremely efficient and bloody boring. That old bridge had character: loose planks that clattered and banged as vehicles drove across; wide railings to lean your elbows on while you scanned the dark-tinted water for fish; even braces you could rest your foot on while enjoying the view.

I was prospecting for early season black crappie the first time I saw the old bridge. The ice had finally left the river, so I decided to check out some areas I had yet to try. When I came to the bridge, I slowed my car on the narrow span and glanced both ways. The water flowing downstream from the swamp to the big river looked interesting — inviting. I pulled off on the wide shoulder of the road, in front of a late-model station wagon.

Downstream, on the right bank, stood what appeared to be a father-and-son fishing team. A young man, perhaps in his late 20s, and a boy about six. The man was casting a small spoon with his spinning outfit, and his son did a passable job of imitating him with one of those little pushbutton spincasting combinations. I leaned over the weathered railing and gazed down at the water. Almost directly below was a stringer of fish. A dozen or so fair-sized crappie were pinned to the chain, but what really attracted my attention was a pike of about five pounds.

"Your fish?" I asked. The young man nodded, but did not look up. "That pike is out of season," I continued. "They don't open for another month."

He looked up, annoyance showing on his face. "You the game warden?"

I shook my head. "No — just a fisherman who reads the regulations."

"Well, I suggest you mind your business, and I'll mind mine."

I shrugged. "Have it your way." I turned and walked back to my car. As I rummaged through the catch-all between the front seats for a pen and notebook, another car pulled off the road at the opposite end of the bridge. From it emerged a short, slender man dressed in tan slacks and a matching windbreaker. As he strolled slowly across the bridge, I saw he was fiftyish, clean-shaven, and had a closely-trimmed moustache that matched his grey hair.

I was busy writing down the licence number of the station wagon when I heard the newcomer say in a pleasant manner, "I'm afraid you're jumpin' the gun on pike season, young fella'. It doesn't open till the second Saturday in May."

"You the game warden?" came the sarcastic reply.

"That's exactly who I am — the deputy conservation officer for this region." The man's friendly demeanour had vanished and the words came out flat and hard. "That pike is illegal. Get it off that stringer — right now!"

The young man moved swiftly to release the captive pike. His face crimson with embarrassment or bad temper — probably both — he lifted his stringer from the water and turned to the boy. "C'mon, let's go." Disappointment showed on the boy's face, but he obediently followed his father up the bank.

As the station wagon drove off, I turned to the stern-faced man. "Nice. You saved me a trip to look up a telephone."

He shook his head slowly. "That little fella' was probably his son. Damn! It makes me mad to see someone flout the law in front of little kids. But your own son?..."

"Well, to be quite honest with you," I said, "I would have ticketed him if I'd been a conservation officer."

"Damned right!" The man nodded his agreement, then grinned. "So would I — if I was really a conservation officer."

BAD RIVER

"We're in business," George Pinchin announced quietly. "You'd better reel in while I battle this monster walleye."

"A good one?"

He chuckled. "They're all good. It feels pretty average, maybe a couple or three pounds."

I finished reeling in, then groped for the flashlight, promptly knocking it off the seat. George had the walleye beside the boat when I finally found it and directed a cone of bright light out into the inky darkness. "Want me to net it?"

"No, it's well hooked. No sense getting it tangled up if we don't have to." He reached out, grasped the line and hoisted the fish into the boat. "Well, I've caught my supper. If you don't want to eat beans tomorrow night, you'd better get busy."

A light flashed close to our right, and we saw Grant Hopkins straining his rod to lead a fish into the net held by Richard Henderson. As he swung it into the boat I called out, "How big?"

"Five and a half," Grant answered. "Maybe six."

"A mere baby," Richard said. "I want him to catch a twin to that fish in the freezer." He was referring to a 12-pound trophy awaiting shipment to a taxidermist. While three pounds shy of the lodge record, it was a fine-looking fish.

Almost simultaneously two other lights illuminated boats farther upstream. "Looks like business is booming," George said. "Let's get in on it."

We doused our light and George slipped the motor into gear. I counted 30 pulls of line from my casting reel, then settled back in the darkness as my seven-inch Rapala pulsed rhythmically about 60 feet behind the boat. The night air was cool and refreshing, and the early July moon provided just enough light for George to thread our way slowly through the maze of rocks and islands cluttering the Bad River's main channel. A few minutes passed, then the rod jerked in my hand. "Well, if I get it in, there's my supper."

We headed in shortly before midnight with four fish averaging 2½ to three pounds — more than enough for Ruth Pinchin's promised fish fry the next evening.

* * * *

Located about 40 air miles south of Sudbury, Ontario, Bad River Lodge nestled on a rugged granite promontory within sight of Lake Huron's Georgian Bay. As it was accessible only by air or water, most visitors chose to be ferried in from the Hartley Bay Marina, a few miles west of the community of French River on Highway 69.

The initial run of about 14 miles was made down the western branch of the French to where it divides into Voyageur Channel and Bad River. The remaining three miles led through a confusion of small islands and narrow, twisting channels. Boaters quickly learned how Bad River got its name, for barely submerged rocks posed a constant threat to propellers.

The entire area has long been popular with landscape artists and photographers. The reason becomes obvious to anyone journeying through this sprawling archipelago of faintly coloured, pastel-pink rock. Large islands wear mantles of dark evergreens, lush mosses, and colourful wildflowers. Below, in areas affected by fluctuating water levels, pale green lichens pattern the exposed rock. While evergreens grow in profusion throughout the protected inland areas, their numbers thin near the lake. Many islands exposed to the open expanse of Georgian Bay have been rounded and worn smooth by wind and water. Lacking soil or nutrients, most are devoid of vegetation, but a few have solitary trees that cling tenaciously to life despite their hostile environment. Stunted, twisted and gnarled, those wind-sculpted evergreens add a surrealistic touch to the area's beauty.

Healthy populations of smallmouth bass, pike and muskie were common throughout the region, but Bad River's main attraction was walleye. Many of the channels and bays were major feeding areas, but much of the action occurred on a half-mile stretch right in front of the lodge. During the summer months, many anglers pursued walleye at night, then concentrated on other species during the day.

The favoured daytime walleye tactic was "controlled drifting," using either a jig-and-worm combination or a worm harness. Similar to backtrolling, the boat drifted downstream stern first, using a bow-mounted electric motor or an idling outboard to manoeuvre over prospective runs. Drift speed was controlled by shifting in and out of gear.

Jigs ranged from ⅛- to ¾-ounce, and most had a "stinger" — trailing hook — attached behind with a short length of monofilament. A large nightcrawler was festooned on the hooks, then lowered to the bottom.

Some multi-hook worm harnesses were unadorned, but the more popular ones sported one or two small spinner blades. They were rigged with an 18-inch leader, a small swivel and a sliding sinker, a setup that was also popular with anglers fishing from shore.

Trolling plugs could be very productive, and like most fishing destinations Bad River had its all-time favourite lure: the original floating Rapala in a silver finish with either a blue or a black back. They ranged in length from four to seven inches, with smaller models preferred for daytime use. Sufficient weight was added to scour the bottom of deep runs, for walleye retire to the gloomy depths during periods of bright sunshine.

Trolling was also the primary night-fishing technique, with large, unweighted Rapalas fished close to the surface, providing a silhouette for walleye to target. As the marauding predators herded baitfish onto shoals or into shallow bays, they could be heard splashing and feeding right on the surface. When this occurred, trollers reeled in and cast slightly beyond the disturbance, then retrieved slowly through it.

* * * *

During my first trip to Bad River in the late 1970s, lodge operator Larry Henderson introduced me to night-trolling. We ventured out for an hour or so, long enough for Larry to land three plump walleye. My identical Rapala attracted nothing, which I attributed to typical Jones luck; however, Larry said it simply needed "fine-tuning" to make it roll more.

The following morning, Larry tested my plug by drawing it through the water as he walked back and forth along the dock. "Definitely not enough roll," he pronounced. "No roll, no walleye — not at night, anyway." Using needle-nose pliers, he bent the wire nose loop slightly downward. When next drawn through the water, the plug's side-to-side roll had increased noticeably, but it took another couple of minuscule adjustments to satisfy him. From that point on, the modified plug produced well during my night-fishing forays.

Anglers seeking pike or bass action usually headed east toward the Fingerboard Islands, or west toward the Chicken Islands. Smallmouths were abundant throughout the entire system, and while some were real bruisers, the average was one to two pounds. They provided steady action on ultralight tackle, which offered a good diversion while anglers waited for an occasional three- to five-pounder to make an appearance.

Nearby Caugee's Bay and Voyageur Channel annually produced a few pike of over 20 pounds, but most were from three to five pounds. Admittedly great sport on light tackle, but frustrating to someone geared up for trophy-sized fish. Casting large spoons and spinners was the most popular tactic, allowing anglers to fish close to weed beds along the edges of deeper water. As weeds provided security and shade for the baitfish, pike usually lurked nearby. The two most popular spinners were large Mepps and Panther Martins, either skirted with squirrel tail or trailing soft plastic minnows. Favoured spoons were the venerable old red-and-white Dardevle, Len Thompson Five of Diamonds, and gold or silver Williams Wablers.

During summer months, the backwaters turned murky and pike became ultra-selective about lure colours. A lure that cleaned up in one bay often a drew blank in another, as was illustrated while I was fishing with Richard Henderson. Everything but the smallest pike avoided my frequently-changed selection of spoons, while Richard's silver Williams Wabler — the only one we had — accounted for several fish up to 12 pounds. Then, when we moved into the next bay, his action ground to an immediate halt while my fluorescent red Dardevle totally reversed the earlier situation.

Many islands and reefs scattered along the Georgian Bay shoreline were proven muskie haunts, but the species received relatively little fishing pressure around Bad River. A few were caught each season by anglers intent on pike, and occasionally bass anglers were shocked by having a toothy leviathan appear from nowhere to swipe a fish while it was being fought. As big muskies favour feeding areas adjacent to fairly deep water, encounters in the relatively warm, shallow bays were usually with smaller fish.

* * * *

It is the tag end of my last morning at Bad River. Larry Henderson lounges in the stern, his rod untouched as he enjoys a cigarette. I cast toward a bed of dense weeds bordering a channel of deep, murky water. My silver spoon lands close beside the growth and starts fluttering downward. The strike is solid, typical of a pike's swift attack, but the heavy, unyielding surge of power that follows is totally unexpected. The reel's drag is nowhere near enough to slow the fish, so I apply firm, hide-warming thumb pressure to the spool. Rod and line strain to their utmost, but the fish continues bulldozing well into the vegetation. My line goes suddenly slack. "Damn!"

Larry shrugs and shakes his head. "Too bad." He holds his hands apart far enough to accommodate well over a yard of fish.

"Pike or muskie?" I ask, tugging and jerking my lure back through the grasping weeds.

"Who cares? It got away, didn't it?" He laughs. "Probably a pike. We don't usually get big muskies this far from the lake."

The soggy ball of weeds is peeled apart, revealing the partially straightened single hook.

"Well?" says Larry, tapping a forefinger on his wristwatch.

I chuckle and slip the point of the damaged hook into my rod's keeper ring. "Okay, Henderson, let's call it quits. I can't think of a better way to end the trip."

WALLEYES

Whether you call them pickerel, pike-perch, dore or walleye, these large members of the perch family have an avid following from British Columbia to Quebec. Although originally present only east of the Rockies, they are now found on the western side, where, after being introduced in Washington state, they eventually worked their way up the Columbia River to the Keenleyside Dam in the Kootenays.

Although they are generally rated as poor fighters, there is a certain mystique about walleyes, and many anglers prefer them over any other species. A schooling fish, they can be as difficult to entice as finicky brown trout, but on other occasions they bite as fast as a jig or baited hook is lowered into the depths. As one fishing partner puts it, the only dependable thing about walleyes is that they are undependable.

Grant Hopkins once wrote to me about fishing in the Ottawa River, where he was "... catching walleye in three feet of water in the middle of a blazing summer day. Nearest deep water at least a mile away. How do you figure that one?" Well, I can't figure it because I'm not a walleye, but it reminded me of a sweltering day on the Rideau River, upstream from Ottawa near Manotick. The tepid water was too murky to see into, but the leadhead jig dangling from the tip of my ultralight spinning rod informed me it was barely two feet deep. As my canoe drifted slowly downstream, I detected a sudden drop to about four feet — and immediately felt a sharp tug on the line. What followed was the wildest, most intensively productive walleye fishing I have ever experienced.

A narrow cleft ran along the river's bottom. No more than five feet wide by about 40 feet long, it was packed with hungry walleyes.

Four feet of water? Bright, glaring sunlight? Walleye? Those opal-orbed fish that shun light? It sounds crazy, but there they were, ranging in size from one to five pounds. Each drift produced a fish, after which I would switch on the electric motor and run back upstream. When the action finally tapered off I had caught 22 walleyes, releasing all but enough for supper.

Even more puzzling, those fish didn't fight like walleyes. When hooked, they rocketed off the bottom and thrashed about on the surface, beating it to a froth. While the one- and two-pounders provided fast action that was totally out of character for the species, those large ones really outdid themselves. Short of actually jumping from the water, they scrapped more like smallmouth bass than anything else. A lot of folks figure that where fighting abilities are concerned, walleye make excellent eating. While I am normally inclined to agree, on occasions like the one just described they have tested my tackle to extremes.

* * * *

Another memorable occasion took place on a late autumn day near Smith's Falls, again on the Rideau. The tiny Rapala plug I was casting for smallmouth bass suddenly stopped as if it had snagged on a rock. I switched on the electric motor and moved my canoe upstream to change the line of pull, which is when the "rock" pulled back. It marked the beginning of a very one-sided tug-of-war. Initially, I thought my lure had been intercepted by a muskie, but at feeling the hook one of those toothy gamesters would have either surfaced or streaked off downstream. Whatever was down there, I quickly discovered that straining on the eight-pound-test line was futile, for the critter simply refused to move.

I finally knelt in the canoe and peered over the side. Despite the water's murkiness, I made out the outline of a big fish on the bottom, but not well enough to determine its species. It didn't appear the least bit disturbed by my actions, so I assumed it was foul-hooked. Rather than prolong the ordeal, I grasped the line in my hand and jerked. Just as the tiny hook straightened and pulled free, the behemoth rolled slowly to one side, revealing the distinct, white-tipped anal fin that identifies members of the walleye family.

That evening, I telephoned Larry Bourgeois and related my encounter. Having worked the weekend he had the next day off, so he made immediate plans to fish that same stretch in the morning. Larry stopped by the following evening to show me his 11-pound walleye — a truly handsome beast that gave me a case of the raging green envies — and to tell me of a 14-pounder taken by another angler. And, of course, to rub it in a bit.

"What chokes me up," I said, "is that the biggest walleye I have ever seen was probably hooked in the mouth — until I intentionally straightened the hook."

Larry studied the beer remaining in his glass for a moment, then replied, "Would it be fair to say that at the precise moment you pulled on the line, there was a tremendous jerk at each end?"

I thought about it for a moment, then nodded and got up to get us another beer. You can't argue with the truth.

HOT FISHING

Louis Skead studied the contents of my open tackle box, then withdrew a ¼-ounce, black-bodied jig. "This looks a bit like a leech. Cast it toward shore and bounce it back along the bottom."

I was doing just that when a fish hit and doubled the rod over in a satisfying arc. Only problem was, it was Louis's rod — and he was using a deep-diving plug: a perch-coloured Shad Rap.

"You snookered me!" I accused.

"No I didn't. You're after bass; this is a walleye." He lifted the bronze-coloured two-pounder from the water and grinned. "Well, I've got my shore lunch."

The day before, after attending an Outdoor Writers of Canada annual convention at Minaki Lodge, Jack Simpson and I drove south to Kenora, then 20 miles west to the marina at Clearwater Bay Landing. There, Roger Clinton met us at the dock, and ferried us about 10 miles to Clinton's Ash Rapids Camp on Sherlock Point.

While Roger skilfully threaded his 21-footer between rocky, tree-covered islands and around barely submerged shoals, Jack explained he was interested in video-taping some bass-bugging sequences for a proposed program about fly-fishing. Roger was dubious. "Early August isn't very good for top-water action — the bass are down about 10 feet or more. Jigs and deep-diving plugs will take them, but leeches are really the ticket. Maybe early, before the sun comes up, or just at dusk...."

Jack smiled. "We realized this was a poor time for surface fishing, but OWC wouldn't change their convention date to accommodate us. Anyway, I need good light to shoot, so early and late are definitely out. We'll fish lures and leeches during the day, but Bob can take his fly rod along and try to work a miracle."

"You should have been here in May or June," said Roger. "It's outstanding for bass, walleye and pike then, and that's when we've got some of the finest black crappie fishing imaginable. Muskies open in late June, but your best chances are after mid-August when the water cools and they get more aggressive. That's when the bass and pike start surface feeding again, too."

"I take it we won't have much competition from the locals if we fish bass?" Jack said.

"None to speak of. They pretty well ignore them."

"So we found out in Kenora." Jack told him of our visit to a tackle shop that morning. When informed we were after smallmouth bass, the clerk asked what part of the United States we were from. After we assured him we were both genuine Canucks, he laughed. "Well, there you go, eh? The Yanks come here for bass, but we fish for walleyes, muskies and lake trout — in about that order of preference."

Roger nodded and chuckled. "That's right, Jack. This whole system is alive with smallmouths, and there's very little pressure on them. Our American guests think they've died and gone to bass heaven when they get here. Some have been coming here for 20 years, long before Gina and I showed up."

The next morning, while Jack and I were eating breakfast at the main lodge, Roger announced that my guide would be Louis Skead. "He can tell you anything you want to know about the area. He was born here during the early 30s, and he's been guiding ever since he was a kid. He's considered the finest 'old time' guide on the lake, a real gentleman." He paused and laughed. "Jack isn't as lucky — he gets me."

With breakfast over, we carried our equipment down to the dock and met Louis. After loading the boats and vowing to stay within camera range of each other, Louis and I headed out in a westerly direction, with Roger and Jack close behind. Scarcely five minutes from the lodge, Louis killed the outboard, lowered an electric motor into the water, then peered into my tackle box....

Shortly after Louis landed his walleye, I felt a sharp tug and set the hook. A chunky smallmouth proceeded to perform most of the things that endear them to anglers: flip-flop jumps, shimmying tail-walks across the surface, and some powerful dives. Louis said the two-pounder was about average. "They run from one to three pounds, but we get fair numbers of four- and five-pounders, too."

As we drifted and cast, Louis described the area's fishing. "From mid-June to mid-July, the bass and walleye usually stay pretty close together, mostly around the rocky points and reefs. The islands and some of the bays with steep drop-offs are good, too. About mid-July the water warms up and they head for deep water, so we have to search for them. Pike are usually along the edges of the weed beds, mostly on the rocky flats between the islands and shallow bays. They'll take top-water plugs in the spring and again in the fall, but Dardevles and Len Thompsons are pretty dependable all through the season."

"How big do they get?"

"Five, 10, 15 pounds, sometimes 20. The muskies get bigger — that one hanging on the lodge wall is 43 pounds."

Smallmouth bass interrupted our conversation at a fairly regular pace, and by noon we had kept enough to contribute our fair share toward the shore lunch. After lunch, at Jack's urging I switched my casting outfit for an 8-weight fly rod and flogged the water to a froth with assorted creations of sculpted deer hair. The only miracle I worked was that of exuding buckets of perspiration without fainting. My efforts yielded one stunted, obviously heat-deranged rock bass found lurking in a shallow, weedy bay where Jack insisted I cast "for some background material."

The following morning there was high overcast and the air was stifling. Roger and Louis decided we would fish southwest through Ash Rapids into Labyrinth Bay, then on down to Shoal Lake. I was relieved to discover Ash Rapids was hardly a raging maelstrom. In fact, the current flowing sedately through the narrow gut between Ash Bay and Labyrinth Bay was barely discernible. It looked fishy though ... very fishy.

Looks can be deceiving. When our lures attracted minimal attention, Louis suggested we try leeches. Rigging my ultralight spinning outfit with a $1/16$-ounce ball-head jig, I hooked a leech lightly through the skin at the head (the end with the suction disc). After lobbing it toward shore, I let it swim downward, then raised the rod tip to lift it slightly above the sloping, rocky bottom some 15 feet below. The first bite took scarcely a minute.

Smallmouths don't smack a leech like they do hardware; they mouth it lightly. Striking immediately usually results in a miss. Better to stop retrieving and lower your rod tip slightly to reduce pressure on the line, or even flip open the bail and release a bit of line. A series of slight tugs and taps may follow, but a wise angler waits until there is a slow, steady pull against the line before striking. This can take anywhere from a few seconds to a half minute or more. Despite the wait, in most cases the bass will be hooked only in the lip.

The moving water below Ash Rapids yielded several nice bass, then we power drifted down Labyrinth Bay with the electric motor. We were just at the entrance of Shoal Lake Narrows when a solid tug on my line resulted in a heavier-than-average fish. It stayed deep and fought stubbornly against the light tackle, but eventually the shape of a large walleye appeared — about six pounds. As I led it toward the boat, Louis reached for the pliers. "That goes back right now."

"Why so?"

"Shoal Lake is closed for walleye." He tugged the hook loose, then cranked the outboard motor into life. As we cruised out of the area, he explained that walleye in the lake had been seriously overfished, so the Ministry of Natural Resources had initiated a total closure to allow their stocks to rebuild naturally.

"Is it working?"

Louis nodded. "There are some big fish down there now, 15 pounds and better. When MNR decides to open it, we'll have the best walleye fishing in the world — for a while. But in the meantime, if I catch one down here, I let it go as quick as I can, then

I move. It isn't worth the hassle if a fisheries officer sees you catch a walleye, even if it's an accident."

That night the storm which had threatened all day finally hit. The camp was pummelled by blinding lightning displays, and thunder so close the concussions were felt as well as heard. Rain drenched the countryside and the wind gusted to gale-force intensity, buffeting our cabin. Then, when the noise and fireworks finally subsided, the night air was cool and we felt comfortable for the first time in several days. By morning, only a few scattered clouds remained overhead and the temperature was still relatively cool. Jack figured the rain might have lowered the lake's surface temperature, so Louis ran me into a small bay with a fairly steep shoreline of broken rock. I started off with the fly rod, but though the calm waters fairly reeked of bass, it produced nothing. "Is this what is referred to as 'flogging a dead horse'?" I yelled at Jack.

He lowered the camera from his shoulder. "Apparently. Roger's starting to doze off, so let's go fishing."

As I stowed the fly rod, Louis said, "You want to come out after supper and try that outfit just as it's getting dark?"

"Louis, you're such a smooth talker. But in the meantime, hand me a leech."

That evening found us back in the narrow, reed-lined bay west of the lodge. Louis was casting a Heddon Dying Flutter, a surface plug with propellers at each end, and I had tied on a deer-hair mouse with a rubber tail. We worked slowly along the northern shoreline, but tempted nothing. It was almost dark when we turned and started up the opposite shore. Louis pointed. "See that rock at the edge of those reeds? I've hit some big bass right beside it."

There was an open pocket of water to the right of the boulder, and more through good luck than skill I dropped my bug in its centre. It lay quietly for several seconds, then a dark shape shot cleanly out of the water beside it, did a half turn and came down on top of the bug. It was a hefty smallmouth that put up a truly memorable scrap before being led to the boat and released. We guesstimated it at 4½ pounds, the largest bass of our trip.

When we finally said our goodbyes to the Clintons and Louis Skead, Jack had taped several hours of "background material": me tossing short lines and long lines, roll casting, double hauling — all in front of picturesque backgrounds. However, despite what probably amounted to several miles of tape being shot, the only fly-caught fish in evidence was that stunted, heat-deranged rock bass. All five inches of it.

WINDFALL

Hotchkiss hesitated by the door and growled, "I'll stop by tomorrow — after work — and you can give me all the sordid details."

I flashed him a patronizing smile. "I'll try not to catch too many, old buddy."

Hotch gave me a withering look and muttered something unintelligible as he stalked out. I doubted that he was wishing me good luck. It would have been nice having him along in the morning, but one does not ignore a windfall day off work during mid-week.

The morning dawned cool and clean-smelling. It had rained off and on for two days, but the skies were clearing. My destination was southeast of the city, a series of deep pools and runs downstream from a water storage dam. Hotch and I fished there often, taking some fine smallmouth bass and walleye, occasionally a bonus muskie.

I arrived at the turn-off to the river, which was hidden by the wooded area bordering it. Two dirt tracks leading down the steep hill looked great at the top, but quickly turned into deep ruts ending at a washout large enough to gobble up a good-sized truck. With no place to turn around, anyone foolish enough to drive down had to attempt backing up the hill. A few with four-wheel-drive vehicles made it if the ground was dry, but if the soil was the least bit damp they would spin out, then end up hiking a quarter mile to the nearest house. There the owner would gleefully phone his neighbour, a farmer who owned a large tractor with a sturdy winch.

I knew better than to drive down the hill. My standard procedure was to nose the front wheels of my van onto the tracks, then back out onto the road and pull well off onto the shoulder. Which I started to do, failing to realize that the rain had made the tracks slippery. Enough so that when I pressed my foot on the brake pedal, the van had just enough momentum to continue sliding forward, wheels dutifully locked. All the way down. Once I was into the deep ruts, steering was futile, but the steering wheel gave me something to hang on to while trying to depress the brake pedal through the metal floorboards onto the axle. After a slow, leisurely descent, the front wheels stopped within inches of the gaping washout.

Knowing it was useless to try backing up the hill, I simply switched off the ignition and got out of my van. As I stepped back on the sloping ground to slam the door shut, my feet suddenly skidded on the wet grass and I crashed heavily onto my right side. I lay there momentarily, the wind knocked out of me, then decided nothing was damaged except my dignity. Which was when I discovered my fall had been cushioned by a very large, very fresh cow patty.

"Ten bucks a tow," the elderly cottage owner cackled. "Jake makes lotsa beer money from that hill." He paused, squinting his rheumy eyes at me. "Jeez, boy, no offence, but yer kinda hummy. Sure clears out the sinuses though."

Later, as the farmer tucked my money into his shirt pocket he said, "River's sure in terrible shape, eh?"

"What?"

"Runnin' pure mud. Bridge crew started dredgin' upstream this mornin'. Guess the fishin's screwed for a day or two, eh?"

"Yeah. I guess it is." I thanked him and climbed into the van. I figured there was plenty of time to drive home, clean up, then have a large tot of single malt before Hotch showed up to find out how my day had gone. Maybe two or three....

A SPECIAL DAY

"I'm going to run right up under the bridge," I informed my bearded companion. Seated in the bow of my 14-foot canoe, Larry Bourgeois nodded, his eyes not wavering from the pulsating tip of his casting rod. I switched the electric motor speed selector to Fast,

then lined up the bow with a channel of swift water flowing beside
the central bridge abutment. From past experience I knew the tiny
power plant was capable — just barely — of moving us upstream
without needing an assistance from the paddle.

"Watch your rod," I cautioned.

Larry glanced over his shoulder at the grey slab of concrete
looming before us, then casually swung his rod out of harm's
way. The motor droned, its tiny propeller churning mere inches
above the rocky bottom. As our bow cleft silently into the
smooth slick that funnelled into the channel, I stood and
scanned the river upstream, where vast weed beds choked the
turbid, slow-moving water.

From his seat in the bow Larry drawled, "Common sense tells me
to reel in."

"Yeah, I...." My reply was cut short when a sudden wrench on my
casting rod pulled me off balance. Purely by reflex, I pivoted sharply
and dropped to my knees on the low, foam-rubber seat. The wild
convulsions telegraphing up the line indicated the fish was probably
well hooked, but I hauled back sharply on my rod just to make sure.
Reaching down, I flicked the speed selector to Slow, then adjusted
the tiller to keep the bow pointed upstream.

Larry cranked furiously on his reel to clear his plug from the
water. "What you got, man — a muskie?"

I shook my head. "No, I don't think so. If it is, it's not very big."

After exchanging his rod for a paddle, Larry said, "Okay, I've got it."

I switched off the motor and flipped it up, clear of the water.
"Let's go, Hiawatha!"

The canoe gained momentum as Larry dug his wide-bladed
paddle into the water, propelling us downstream under the bridge.
Within moments we were through the channel, where the river
widened and the current slowed. Larry feathered his paddle, nosing
the stern into a quiet backwater.

Having retrieved line during our downstream journey, I now felt
the fish's dogged attempts to free itself coming from upstream.
Confident of my tackle, I snubbed the spool tightly with my thumb
and strained on the rod. The fish turned and suddenly streaked
toward us. My hand was a blur of motion as I cranked frantically,

trying to keep the line tight. As a dark form rocketed beneath the canoe, I detected a telltale glimpse of white in the gloom.

"Walleye!" I swung the rod around the stern, then twisted in the seat to face the fish. "Looks like a fair-sized one," I said as the fish sounded, dragging my rod tip well under the surface.

It was a strong fight from a fish that had obviously never read the books claiming "walleye are not aggressive fighters." With the exception of jumping, it tried every tactic in the book; however, the steady pressure from my rod and reel eventually took its toll. The bronze beauty rose slowly from the depths toward the waiting net, a classic example of the species: 5½ pounds of burnished brown and gold, set off by a deep belly as unblemished and creamy-white as polished ivory.

We released most of the fish we caught, but drew the line at walleye — better to throw away a prime T-bone in our estimation than release a respectable-sized walleye. I killed the fish with a sharp blow to the head, then placed it beneath a damp burlap sack. It was only slightly larger than a fat, beautifully marked pike Larry had taken earlier in the day. Although admittedly small for that species, it had swallowed his plug so deeply that major surgery was required to recover the hooks.

"Well," I said, "what say we look for some brothers and sisters?"

"You're the captain."

As I lowered the motor and switched the selector to Fast, Larry snapped a precise cast within inches of the shoreline. We were both using floating Rapalas, his a gold, black-backed 5 ¼-inch model, mine a silver, light blue-backed seven-incher.

When I cast toward the opposite bank, a vagrant gust of wind caught my plug, causing it to suddenly pause in flight. I muttered a few appropriate words, then began picking at the snarled line on my spool.

"Is that what's commonly referred to as a 'backlash'?" Larry asked.

"Sarcasm, young man, is the indication of a diseased mind."

He cackled and slapped his knee. "Hey! That's good. Can I have it for work?"

"It's yours," I said as the last loop pulled free.

A few minutes later the Sportspal once more crept slowly upstream past the bridge abutment, and within inches of my earlier strike I felt the savage jolt of another fish smashing into my plug. I struck back sharply on the already-straining rod, and the waters beneath the bridge erupted in an explosion of spray as a large fish thrashed wildly on the surface.

"Fish hog," Larry growled, once more cranking his lure free of the battleground.

I grinned, thinking of the many times the shoe had been on the other foot. "I do believe a nasty old muskie has got me on the line."

The fish suddenly ceased its eggbeater tactics and raced downstream, quartering toward a large weed bed. My hand grabbed for the tiller and swung the motor through a full 180 degrees. The canoe, which had been barely moving upstream, suddenly changed direction and picked up momentum. As I struggled to lift the motor clear of the water, my partner's voice informed me he once more had control of the situation. Even as we shot through the fast water, my reel continued squalling while line ripped from its spool.

"It thinks it's a bloody steelhead making a run like that!" I exclaimed, trying to slow the rush by adding thumb-pressure —very carefully — on the spool. Within a few feet of the weed bed's sanctuary, for some inexplicable reason the muskie made an abrupt turn and charged back toward us. I cranked furiously, trying to recover slack line as the fish drew nearer. Less than 10 feet from the gunwale, it hurtled into the air in a magnificent, water-clearing jump. It hung suspended against the cloudless blue sky for just a moment, then crashed back in a geyser of water.

"Hey!" Larry yelped. "No visitors in the 'Tin Goose,' eh!"

I didn't blame him. It was a gut-wrenching feeling to sit with my butt at water level, looking up at that muskie and wondering if I was going to be wearing it. Twice more it vaulted from the water, but neither leap was as high or as spectacular as its first jump. The battle seemed to swing my way, even though that fish tried most of the tricks associated with the *Esox* clan: sounding deep to rub the lure along bottom; rolling in the line; and continually darting under the canoe, making it necessary for me to plunge my rod tip deep into the water to keep the line from fouling.

A greenish-brown back broke through the surface as the fish's strength finally waned. I reached out cautiously with my left hand, then firmly clamped thumb and fingers over its gill covers. Placing the rod handle between my knees, I grabbed my needle-nose pliers off the lid of my tackle box. Heaving the fish's head onto the gunwale, I gripped the hook jutting from its upper jaw and quickly tugged it free.

"What do you figure?" Larry asked.

I strained to lift the fish at arm's length — easier said than done from my sitting position. "Not gross. Sixteen, maybe a bit better."

The irregular, olive-coloured pattern that differentiates muskies from their pike cousins was quite faint, almost obscured by the glowing, pewter-like sheen of its sides, and its large, translucent-orange fins contrasted sharply with the white of its belly.

"Hang on while I get a picture," Larry said, adjusting the settings on his camera.

The fish chose that moment to find its second wind. It started writhing, so I lowered it quickly into the water and released my grip. A vigorous swipe of its tail catapulted a gallon or so of tepid water into my downturned face as it shot away to freedom. "Sorry about that," I spluttered, grinning through the water streaming from my face.

Larry shrugged. "I just wanted to have some proof — for when you start telling everybody about the 25-pounder you let go." Jabbing his thumb toward the bridge, he said, "What say we anchor below the abutment and try casting into your 'honey hole' for a while?"

I ran our canoe into the shallow water Larry had indicated, then we anchored from each end to prevent it from swinging. My companion overhanded his rod in a casual, fluid motion that delivered his plug with maddening precision, inches from the rocky shoreline. I side-armed an upstream cast directly under the bridge. The water was shallow, so I allowed my lure to float downstream a few feet before jerking it under the surface. It had only moved a short distance when a sharp jar announced the arrival of another fish.

"Will you stop!" Larry complained. "You're giving me a complex."

"Want to hold my rod?"

His answer was unkind and derogatory. The roughhouse struggle that ensued yielded a 4½-pound walleye. Another welcome candidate for the frying pan.

Now a good yarn would end with my companion and me knee-deep in a canoe filled with walleye, but this is a fish story, not a fairy tale. The truth is, we beat the water to a froth for over an hour with nary another nudge to reward our efforts. Not even a rock bass. But that's fishing — either feast or famine — and that's what makes it interesting.

Over five hours in the confines of the canoe brought us to the mutual conclusion that it was time to head home and stretch our legs. We couldn't complain, for our day had been interesting. We had caught and released a parade of smallmouth bass, from tiny tiddlers to a few nudging three pounds, and a few juvenile muskies and pike had struck at our big lures. We were always amazed at their impudence in tackling plugs nearly as large as themselves.

Later, as Larry finished lashing the canoe to the roof rack of my car, I strolled over to the steep bank overlooking the spot where we had landed a few minutes earlier. Amber-tinted waters chuckled musically over the rocky shallows, glittering and twinkling as tumbling wavelets reflected the late afternoon sun. On the small island at mid-channel, a regiment of velvety-brown cattails nodded drowsily on slender green stalks while an errant breeze slowly inspected their ranks.

The end of a day's fishing is a time for reflection, a time to pause, recall the day's events, then file them carefully away among memories gathered previously. Whether Fate was kind or fickle is of little consequence, for the physical act of catching fish should be viewed as merely an exciting aside, not the main theme.

That particular day had a special meaning, for it was to be my last on the Rideau River for a few seasons. A few days later I would leave Ottawa to start a three-year posting at Baden-Soellingen, Germany. Although looking forward to renewing old acquaintances from my previous tour of duty there, I had some regrets about leaving. Larry materialized by my side, but remained silent. My reverie concluded, I sneaked a sidelong glance at him. "Hey, uncivil servant, how 'bout buyin' the old master corporal a beer?"

"Yep." He draped his arm around my shoulder. "I just happen to know where there's a whole fridge full of the stuff — at your place."

THE REVENGE OF MERTON

Merton and Gertrude have a summer cottage on Georgian Bay, about 150 miles north of their home on the outskirts of Toronto. Well, perhaps "tiny cabin" is a better description. It's his wife's idea; Mert would rather have blown a bundle on a large boat, which he could leave in their driveway. Then he could spend all of his spare time and money working on it instead of driving 300 miles round trip to do the same thing with their cottage. He also points out there are fewer blackflies and mosquitoes in their driveway than on Georgian Bay. Nevertheless, once spring weather gets serious, he joins thousands of other city-bound residents on Friday evening, bumper-to-bumper, northward migrations which usually last until long after nightfall.

By the time they arrive, Mert's nervous system is approaching self-destruct, but two fingers of Highland nectar are enough to loosen him up a bit. Two more make him downright sociable. That's because he uses the distance between his index and little finger.

Another problem with Mert's hideaway is his neighbour, Ripley, who consistently catches more and larger walleye than anyone else. He fishes alone, usually at night, and being unsociable to the point of offensiveness, never talks to anyone, let alone shares any secrets of his success. Naturally, whenever Ripley heads out on the water, dozens of binoculars and telescopes are trained on him. Which is how word got around that he trolled seven-inch original Rapalas, upon which he sprayed something. What he sprayed was anyone's guess, because he wrapped black tape around the aerosol can, obscuring the label.

One day, about mid-afternoon, Ripley was fishing for smallmouths when a large muskie inhaled his little bucktail jig. "Large" meaning 50 pounds, according to Mert, who was fishing nearby. In the excitement that followed, Ripley stood up, lost his balance, and pitched overboard, banging his head on the gunwale. Mert immediately cranked his outboard to life, and was dragging the sputtering angler into his boat before scarcely a minute had passed.

"Are you okay?" asked Mert.

"Don't be stupid!" Ripley snarled. "I smacked my head, damned near drowned, and lost my fishin' outfit!"

"Just thought I'd ask," Mert said quietly.

"Run me alongside my boat," Ripley demanded. "I gotta get into some dry clothes."

Mert did as ordered, then steadied their boats while Ripley clambered aboard his, started the outboard and departed without so much as a thank you. Mert sat there for a moment, looking down at the can of scent he had plucked from Ripley's boat. He sprayed a bit onto his fingertips. WD40!

Mert had a fair idea of where Ripley had dropped his rod, so he slid the eye of a large treble hook over his jig hook and started probing the depths.

That evening, Mert paddled his canoe over to Ripley's dock, eased up beside his boat and quickly slipped the tape-wrapped can into it. "Hey! Ripley!" he yelled. "You awake?"

Ripley appeared at the door. "What?"

"I dredged up your fishin' outfit," Mert said. "The jig's gone, but everything else is okay." He placed the rod and reel in Ripley's boat, then paddled home.

Mert was sitting out in their screened porch when a pinpoint of light bobbed down Ripley's trail toward his dock. Shortly afterward his outboard motor coughed quietly to life and his boat's silhouette cruised slowly across the calm, moonlit bay. A few minutes later, the sound of cursing and swearing wafted over the water and Mert smiled. Ripley had obviously just sprayed his Rapala, and probably his hand and other assorted items, with black paint.

§SIX
THE TRAVELLING ANGLER

ODDS AND ENDS

This tale of a streamer fly bounces around somewhat because of its varied and interesting history. While some parts of this account might occasionally appear to stretch the truth a bit, I assure you they are all factual. After all, if you can't trust an angler, who can you trust?

To begin our tale, let's actually start somewhere toward the end of it, say about October of 1975....

Gatwick airport. The big military Boeing 707 jet had landed on British soil a few minutes earlier, disgorging from its crowded interior a mix of tired and rumpled Canadian Forces personnel, civil servants, school teachers, and assorted spouses and children. There was a one-hour layover, time enough to enjoy a cool beer or two before proceeding to Germany. Which is precisely what I was doing when a slim, neatly-dressed sergeant stopped beside my table and asked if the empty chair beside me was taken. As he sat down, he enquired rather hesitatingly, "Didn't you used to be Bob Jones?"

I stared at him for a moment, then laughed. "Yes, about 15 years and 30 pounds ago."

"I'm Bill MacArthur."

"I know! Bill, so help me, you can believe it or not, just yesterday I was telling friends in Ottawa all about you."

He looked puzzled for a moment, then his eyes lit with understanding. "I'll bet it was that damned fly!"

"That's right. You know, after all this time, it's still one of my favourite fishing yarns."

Now, let's move this story back to the early 1960s, in Comox, B.C. A group of avid fishermen is sitting in the Lorne Hotel beer parlour, sipping beer and swapping the latest fishing stories. Bill arrives, pulls a chair over to the gap that is widened for him, sits down and signals the waiter for a round. After the preliminary greetings and friendly insults, the newcomer is asked the inevitable question: "Been on the water?"

"Boys," he answers, "have I got a tale of woe to tell you. I was up on the Puntledge last Saturday morning and hooked into the nicest steelhead I've seen in many moons. Must have gone 11 or 12 pounds if it went an ounce. And a nice bright fish, too.

"I hooked her in that rock cut below the diversion dam, and by the time she was finished racing around and jumping all over the place, we were better than a hundred yards downstream. The best fight I've had from any fish on the Island. Well, boys, just about the time I figure I've got her calmed down enough to think about landing her, doesn't she put on a final burst and foul the leader on a rock or something. And that was it, game over."

There is a moment of silence as we contemplate his story. Not out of respect, simply to search for flaws that might trip up what could prove to be just another "fishing fancy." It rings true, however, so Gino McClean clears his throat and asks, "What did you hook her on, Bill?"

"A queer-looking little bucktail. One I made up with odds and ends from my fly-tying kit. You know, all those little bits and pieces that are too short to use, but too nice to throw away.

"It had a red tail, kind of a golden yellow body, a white bucktail wing and a brown hackle. The funny thing about it was the tinsel. I had a wide piece tied in at the tail, and when I tried to wrap it around the body, it was too short. Well, that stuff doesn't stretch worth a hoot, so I had to settle for pulling it forward to make one long wrap in order to have enough left over to tie it off. Well now, didn't it turn out to be a holy terror on cutthroat down around the river mouths? You know, boys, I think I hated to lose that fly almost as much as the fish."

While Bill was talking, I had reached into my hip pocket and withdrawn my battered old wallet. I probed into one of the plastic compartments to spread it open, then shook a rather flattened streamer fly into the palm of my hand. Picking it up by the hook point, I held it toward Bill. His eyes widened in shocked disbelief, for it was the very fly he had just described.

"Wha!... Where in hell did you get that?" he demanded, reaching toward it.

I snatched the fly away and replied, "Out of a fish's mouth, Bill. Up on the Puntledge. In that rock cut below the diversion dam. This morning."

Bill ran his fingers through his blond hair. "I don't believe it! I just don't bloody believe it!"

"There's just one thing, Bill: you must have really fought that poor old fish to a frazzle before you lost her."

"How so?"

"Because when I caught her this morning, she only weighed about seven pounds. That means she lost four pounds in three days."

After the laughter and catcalls died down, Bill allowed that he might have misjudged the fish's size just a bit during the heat of battle. "But how can you be sure," he concluded, "when the damned things won't stay still long enough for you to get a good look at 'em?"

After a few minutes of table-side bartering, Bill's "Odds and Ends" fly became mine in exchange for two glasses of beer.

* * * *

The next event of note occurred on a hot August day about a year later. Andy McWilliams and I had spent several hours pounding the waters of the Gold River in search of what we came to believe was a mythical run of summer steelhead. Finally admitting defeat, we broke down our casting outfits, crawled wearily into my car, then started the dusty drive back toward Campbell River. As we rolled slowly along the logging road's smooth gravelled surface, Andy pointed to his right, where a thin ribbon of bright water threaded its way through an unsightly mess of tangled and broken timber scattered along the valley bottom. "What's the name of that river again?" he asked.

"Heber. Roderick Haig-Brown wrote about it quite a bit in *Fisherman's Fall.* In fact, I got the impression it was his favourite stream. Must have looked a lot different before the loggers got at it."

"Pretty sad sight isn't it?" Andy said.

"Sad isn't the word. 'Criminal' is more like it. They won't even leave a strip of trees along the banks to offer some semblance of protection from the sun."

"You suppose there's any fish in it?" he wondered aloud.

"I doubt if there's enough water in there to keep a bullhead's belly wet. I suppose we could go down and take a look though."

I slowed and turned the car around, then doubled back until we found an old logging trail offering access by foot through the tangled slash. As we readied ourselves for the hike down into the valley, I decided to take my fly rod instead of the lightweight bait-casting outfit I had used earlier. Figuring we were on a wild goose chase, I thought a bit of fly-casting practice would be a good way to kill time while Andy satisfied his curiosity.

While making our way toward the river, we spotted a fair-sized pool that looked as devoid of life as a swimming pool. "Why don't you go up where that little waterfall comes in at the head?" I suggested. "I'll stay here at the tail and amuse myself."

As Andy made his way upstream, I jointed my two-piece rod and pulled the hook, leader and line through the guides. The last time I had used it, I had been too lazy to remove the fly and store it in the fly box. It was the original tied by MacArthur.

The leader, nothing more than six feet of four-pound-test monofilament, had a tight wind knot about 10 inches from the hook. Much too tight to pick out, but with no fish in that antiseptic-looking pool, I didn't worry about it.

I stood right at the water line and stripped line from the reel, allowing it to fall in loose coils at my feet. As I lifted my rod tip the line followed obediently, and I selected a large rock near the opposite bank to serve as a rising trout. A few false casts lengthened the airborne line, then a final cast forward shot my fly within a foot or so of the target. Not bad. I know a few people who can drop their flies into a coffee cup at 30 feet with disgusting regularity, but I am satisfied if they land somewhere in the general vicinity without any serious mishap.

Just as my fly settled on the water, there was a flicker of movement to my right as a tiny, grey, thrush-like bird made a swooping arrival at the pool's tail. It was a dipper, one of my favourite creatures. I paused to watch the bobbing, bowing antics of the busy bird as it flitted from rock to rock, searching the water for tidbits. Then, as suddenly as it arrived, it was gone, darting back downstream in a low, unswerving flight to seek better pickings.

I reached up idly toward the stripping guide of my rod and grasped the line. A steady pull downward and to the rear swept my now sunken fly up off the bottom, at the same time breaking the floating line's surface tension on the water in preparation for the back cast. I started to lift my rod tip, but about the 10 o'clock position the handle was nearly wrenched from my hand. The pool's quiet surface erupted as a nickel-bright steelhead as long as my arm executed a series of four high-flying leaps. Immediately displaying the skill and dexterity accumulated after long years of angling experience, I stood transfixed, my lower jaw hanging down around my belt buckle, watching that crazy fish do pretty well as she pleased. I finally snapped out of my somnolent state when she attempted to run out of the pool.

As I stumbled after her, displaying the grace and agility of a one-legged grasshopper, all I could think about was the wind knot in my leader — an insidious little knot which I knew all too well had effectively reduced the breaking strain of that slender strand of monofilament by 50%.

The fish streaked down the pool like a torpedo, only to find its already meagre depths ended in a cul-de-sac of large boulders with tiny trickles of water running between them. With no escape there, she turned and raced back into the dubious safety of the pool. Pirouetting gracefully like an overweight ballerina, I staggered, then fell heavily onto my well-padded prat. My tail bone connected solidly with a granite slab, whereupon my entire body was suddenly electrified with that numb, helpless feeling that accompanies a rapped funny bone. As I writhed about in mortal agony, trying to think of something more appropriate to say than "Oww, oww, oww," the fish steamed up the pool, punctuating her progress with two more flashy jumps. I struggled to my feet and hobbled painfully after her.

Despite the steelhead's attempts to rid herself of the hook, she eventually lay spent at my feet. As I pried the bedraggled fly from the side of her lower jaw, I looked up at Andy and stated, "I kneel here before you, living proof that bad management, terminal stupidity and the total lack of co-ordination can all be overcome by a stroke of good luck."

* * * *

Half a world away from Vancouver Island, in the rugged country formerly known as Yugoslavia, the Plitvice Lakes are cradled in a deep valley that cleaves through Plitvice National Park. There, 16 tiny lakes formed steps down the valley, each on its own level, like an emerald jewel wearing a necklace of foaming white waterfalls at its base. After a lifetime of travel to various regions of the world, I still rank it as one of the most beautiful places I have ever seen.

I was with a small group of Yugoslavian and German anglers, part of a larger group which included three other Canadian military personnel who had been invited to take part in the 1971 International Fishing Competition. Our guide for the outing was Dr. Kresimir Paxur, a well-known and highly respected fisheries biologist from Zagreb. An ardent angler, he was an accomplished fly-caster and a master fly-tier.

"There are rainbow and brown trout in all the lakes," the biologist explained, "but there are only three where fishing is allowed." He was speaking in German, the language in which we could all get along — on my part with varying degrees of hand-waving, grimacing, and frequent page-turning of my English-German dictionary.

"This is a good time to use dry flies," he continued. "But where we will be fishing, on Lake Ciginovac, there is no room to use fly rods. What I suggest is that you all use spinning tackle with small plastic bobbers."

In stumbling German, I explained that I had a five-foot-long midge rod which might work despite the thick foliage. Dr. Paxur smiled. "Of course, Herr Jones. I too enjoy experimenting on strange waters with my own equipment and methods. Perhaps if you explore along the far shore you will find a spot where you can cast."

The lake was shaped like the letter V, with us at the converging end. I made my way along the well-groomed pathway skirting the shoreline, and found myself opposite my companions before locating a suitable spot. A slender finger of flat rock jutted about four feet out from shore. Behind and slightly to its right was a narrow cleft in the solid wall of overhanging tree branches. Not the greatest casting platform in the world, but enough that I could roll cast without too much difficulty.

I opened my aluminum fly box and studied the contents to determine what treasures were hidden in its overlapping rows of feather, fur and tinsel. There in the lower corner lay Odds and Ends. Over 10 years old, it was somewhat chewed up but still weathering the years fairly well. Scattered throughout the box were offspring I had patterned after the original, and productive flies they were. But for some reason they never captured my fancy quite like their sire. I knew the fly was far too large for my small rod, but for some perverse reason I plucked it from the box and knotted it onto my leader.

My first cast was definitely not the sort one brags about. At best, roll casting with a five-foot rod limits one; attempting it with a fly some six sizes too large made it next to impossible. Ideally, my fly would have gracefully followed the rolling line's direction. Instead, it shot straight forward at a low trajectory, then plunged onto the mirrored surface with a loud splat. I was thankful that Dr. Paxur, who held a few European fly-casting titles, was not close enough to observe my crude attempts.

The fly floated for a moment, then slowly submerged. Although it was scarcely 15 feet away, I decided to let it sink, then fish it in. I started mentally counting to 10, which would help me gauge the water's depth, and determine at which level the fish were suspended — in the event that one saw fit to take my offering. My count on the next cast would be 15, followed by 20, until I found either bottom or a fish.

It turned out there·was no need to pursue my countdown, for at three a sudden bulge appeared just below the surface as my fly was intercepted by a brown trout which appeared to be swimming slightly under the speed of sound. The tiny rod came alive in my hand, and the reel whirred as line streamed from its spool. The sound carried over the water, so Dr. Paxur hurried along the pathway to see what all the fuss was about.

By the time he arrived, I had subdued the fish — about two pounds — and released it. However, just as he appeared on the scene, a twin to the first fish nailed my sinking fly. It was the second of four fish I caught before we had to call it a day, all brown trout of equal size and agility, all taken on the Odds and Ends.

On the return trip to our hotel in Samobor, I offered Dr. Paxur a selection of Odds and Ends in varying sizes. He accepted them gratefully, then bolstered my own collection with several dainty, beautifully-fashioned dry flies which he had tied.

* * * *

Bill MacArthur hoisted the mug to his mouth and took a long drink. Licking the foam from his upper lip, he asked, "Have you still got the darned thing — after all this time?"

"Yep. But I finally quit using it a couple of years ago. I was fishing a little stream in Quebec, in behind Buckingham, the last time it was in the water. That was quite a little stream — I used to get brookies, browns and rainbows all out of the same water. They were pretty well all stocked fish that didn't go much more than nine or 10 inches on the high side of average, but once in a while we'd hit a holdover of up to 14 inches or so. Nice fish. One of the locals told me there were some huge browns in the five- and six-pound range in a few of the deeper holes, but I never put too much stock in it. I was just as happy catching the little ones on dry flies as going after the big ones.

"Anyway, I was prowling around one day and ended up well down-stream on a stretch I'd never tried before — a fair-sized pool at the base of some steep rapids that dumped out in a small waterfall. The water was real dark, that black-looking tinge you find around beaver dams. I figured if I was ever going to run into one of those monster browns I'd heard about, this was the place.

"Well, I drifted a dry fly over that pool a half-dozen times and never got a sniff. I decided a wet or streamer would serve the purpose, so out comes my fly box, and there's your old fly sitting there, sayin', 'Pick me! Pick me!' I tied it on and spit on it so it would sink fast. I figured if there was a big brownie in the pool, it would either be right up against the fast water, or else down near the tail. In order to cover the pool in one drift, I plunked the fly right into the little waterfall at the head. The line went tight right away, and I figure I'd snagged a rock. I lifted the rod, then all of a sudden the snag pulls back and takes off downstream. The way that thing bulldozed down the pool, I figure old Bob has hooked himself the granddaddy of all brown trout, but I can't see anything because of the water. Then all of a sudden the line went kind of slack, and I knew it was going to jump. And it did."

I paused to refresh myself with a swallow of beer. Bill was leaning forward, an intent look on his face. "Well, what was it?" he demanded.

"About four pounds of the blackest-looking smallmouth bass I've ever seen."

"A bass! Did you land it?"

"Nope. It shook loose on that first jump. And that was the last time I used the fly. I went home that evening and locked it away in a drawer in my fly-tying cabinet. A case of 'Lead us not into temptation'."

* * * *

When my military meandering ended in 1980, Vera and I moved back to Vancouver Island. Even now, after all these years, whenever I amuse myself by binding gaudy little patches of hair and plumage to assorted hooks, I see old Odds and Ends on a shelf, nestled safely in its clear plastic container. We are both well past our prime, but I fear it shows more on yours truly than on the fly. On occasion I wonder whether this is the proper way to treat the old fish-deceiver — keeping it tucked away like a treasured lock of hair from the first-born. Maybe I should slip it back into a fly box and wait until I chance upon a particularly fishy-looking steelhead run. I will dig it out and tie it carefully to the leader — checking for wind knots, of course — and cast it out over the water, dropping it right where it will get the best drift. Then I'll let it sink as I slowly start to counting to myself....

FLY-CASTING VS FLY-FISHING

A half-dozen local anglers watch in appreciative awe as Roger MacNeil lays out long, sinuous casts over the shallow end of a *baggersee* (flooded gravel pit) near the RCAF base at Baden-Soellingen, Germany. An Atlantic salmon fisherman from Cape Breton, Nova Scotia, Roger was raised on fly-fishing and it shows. He is the epitome of rhythmic grace as his nine-foot rod lifts the ivory-coloured line into high, tight-looped back casts, then propels it forward over the water, where the leader unfurls smoothly and his dry fly settles gently as a snowflake on the surface. To use a time-worn phrase: Roger is pure poetry in motion.

A hundred yards up the shoreline, I appear to be fighting off a swarm of angry wasps with my fly rod. I am perched where the dredge bucket had scooped deep into the gravel deposited by the Rhine River eons before. The high bank plunges steeply into 30 feet of water, and my footing on the loose rocks and gravel is precarious. Exposed tree roots and overhanging branches make back casting impossible, so I am attempting to roll cast. Properly done, roll casting is quite elegant: the rod tip is lifted slowly upright, drawing line smoothly across the surface toward you. When the lifted portion of line sags almost parallel to the vertical rod shaft, a sharp downward movement of your forearm pushes the rod tip forward and down. Power is transmitted from the rod to the line, whereupon the airborne portion travels outward above the line still remaining on the water, lifting it smoothly upward in a continuous curve that uncoils across the surface, then terminates with the fly gently alighting at the end of your fully extended leader. Honest. All of this happens precisely as described if your timing is right. At the time, mine isn't.

There is no room to lift my rod vertically, and a tiny sphere of lead is pinched midway up the leader's tippet. One or the other is enough to inhibit efficient roll casting; combined, they defeat it. The line sounds like cloth tearing as it rips off the surface. Instead of travelling outward in a continuous airborne coil, it barely clears the water in a dogleg-shaped curve that ends when my fly plops down noisily, barely 20 feet away. If I am lucky. Which I am about one cast out of three. Or four.

One of the Germans watching Roger is my fishing companion, Eduard Boemches, an experienced and efficient angler. A fellow standing beside him comments, "The MacNeil is a very good fly-fisher, but the Jones is very bad."

Ed replies, "Ahh ... but the MacNeil is not catching trout, and the Jones is."

I relate this vignette to illustrate the difference between fly-casting and fly-fishing. Roger had intentionally picked the shallow end of the *baggersee* because its shoreline was flat and devoid of obstructions. There he could indulge in the sheer joy of making his fly line do whatever he wished: precise casts close in; beautifully timed roll casts that scarcely caused a ripple on the surface; or hauling and double-hauling to speed up his line and shoot it out 80 feet or more. No one would have been more surprised than Roger had one of the stocked rainbows or brown trout swum up from the cool, comfortable depths into that warm, shallow water to take his fly.

Miserable and uncomfortable as my location was, I, too, had selected it intentionally, then further complicated matters by pinching on the split shot. I knew from previous experience that the trout were deep, and that a sunken Carey Special retrieved slowly, just above the steep bottom, would trigger strikes. Which came with satisfying regularity, although I kept no fish.

Trying to decide who had more fun would be like making the common taste comparison between apples and oranges. We both enjoyed ourselves. I must admit, however, that Roger's skilful casting display did more to create interest in fly-fishing than did the fact that I caught far more trout that day.

NORTH, BEYOND LA RONGE

From the way Ron Cojocar leaned back on his bowed casting rod, he was into one big pike. As George McKenzie carefully jockeyed our boat into position for me to take photographs, I called out the obvious question, "How big?"

"Hard to say," Ron answered. "Haven't had that good a look yet. Eighteen, maybe 20."

"Well, I've got my camera ready — make it jump."

"Har-de-har, very funny. On 10-pound test I can't make it do anything. If it runs for that bloody weed bed, I'm sunk." He continued pumping and reeling, slowly gaining line, only to lose it again as the fish bulldozed back toward the depths.

Suddenly, the fish turned and raced for the weed bed. It looked like game over, but right at the edge of the dense vegetation the pike veered, and the surface boiled from the turbulence. For the first time the fish showed itself, lunging half out of the water, gill covers and tooth-studded jaws agape, spray flying as its head shook from side to side. It was, indeed, one big pike. However, the unrelenting pressure from Ron's tackle finally took its toll, and the fish was led toward the waiting net. As Gerard Makuch scooped it up and heaved it over the gunwale, Ron spread his arms and whooped for joy.

* * * *

A week earlier, on September 8, our La Ronge Aviation Beaver had skimmed low over an evergreen-covered island and touched down smoothly on the glassy surface of a Churchill River backwater. The 45-mile flight north from La Ronge had carried us over a mosaic of land and water that lent graphic credibility to Saskatchewan's claim of having over 100,000 lakes.

One need only look at a road map of Saskatchewan to appreciate the fishing potential offered by the Churchill River. It originates at Buffalo Narrows, near the Alberta border, and flows eastward through the upper reaches of central Saskatchewan into Manitoba, eventually draining into Hudson Bay. It is a sprawling, cluttered confusion of branches and channels, and while many expanses are far more lake-like than riverine there is always a current.

We were headed for Beyond La Ronge Lodge, located near the northeastern corner of Lac La Ronge Provincial Park. The lodge perches on Mountain Portage, which bypasses the seething white waters of Twin Falls, the main drainage points from Otter Lake into Mountain Lake.

Earlier, during our flight north from Saskatoon to La Ronge, Gerard had explained that during late spring and early summer, thousands of spawning walleye gather in the turbulent water at the base of each falls. When the spawning run ends, they school up and disperse throughout the system.

Saskatchewan boasts 68 species of fish, but those we sought were two of the favourites: walleye and pike. "The Churchill system stays cold the year round," Gerard explained, "so the fish don't seem to get terribly large — but they are really abundant. The walleyes average two to three pounds, but even this late in the season we might find some hitting four pounds. There are a few five- and six-pounders caught every year, but they're considered real trophies for this system.

"There are some respectable pike too — 20 to 25 pounds — but there are so many four- and five-pounders that you have a hard time keeping them off."

I thought of the lightweight casting outfit stored with my luggage and smiled. I could live quite nicely with four- and five-pounders.

As our airplane taxied beside the dock, lodge owner Ron Cojocar was waiting to greet us. While I was easing down onto the pontoon, he said, "Welcome to Beyond La Ronge Lodge. Too bad you couldn't come up when the fishing was hot."

I looked up at Gerard. "Don't get out — he says the fishing's no good."

"Not true," Gerard answered. "The fishing's always good on the Churchill — but it's even better in the summer."

"That's right," said Ron. "If you'd come in July it would have been outstanding. You could have caught walleye right around the corner at the falls, but now you'll have to hunt for them." The original suggestion had been for me to visit in July, but I was tied up with previous writing commitments for the entire summer. As a result, Gerard and I could not make it until early September.

Ron shook his head and looked up at the gathering clouds. "We're expecting a front to hit this evening, so you might end up fishing in a snowstorm before the week's over."

After a hurried lunch of sandwiches and coffee, Gerard and I rigged our tackle, then bundled into heavy parkas and warm boots. Ron ushered us down to the dock and introduced us to our guide for the afternoon, John Roberts.

Our young companion swiftly navigated the 16-foot aluminum boat through a jumbled maze of small islands and narrow channels, barely avoiding submerged rocks and shoals with the sort of casual indifference bred by years of experience. As the boat twisted and turned on its tortuous path, I marvelled at our surroundings. Up to that point, my experience with Saskatchewan had been restricted to southern climes — long stretches of highway cleaving through gently rolling expanses of prairie farmland, ribbons of asphalt that seemed straight-edged beyond the horizon into infinity. Not this roadless tract of wilderness: the rocky islands choking the waterway were covered with tall, straight evergreens that provided a dark, contrasting background for the brilliant autumn yellows and golds of white birch, poplars and willows. It was truly beautiful country.

Scarcely 10 minutes from the dock, John cut the power and our boat mushed to a stop. As Gerard and I dropped identical yellow, soft-plastic-bodied jigs over the side, my fishing partner asked, "Buck on the first fish?"

"You're on." The words were hardly out of my mouth when Gerard swept his rod up to set the hook on our first walleye. A sharp tug announced interest being shown in my own jig, but it was a dollar too late. I had just set the hook when Gerard flipped a three-pounder over the gunwale. Moments later, mine turned out to be a twin. They were beautiful fish with burnished brass-coloured sides and fat, white bellies.

Within an hour we had eight walleyes of two to three pounds in the fish box. While there weren't keeper-sized fish waiting with open mouths every time our jigs were lowered, we stayed busy with smaller walleyes, a few slender saugers that might have gone 16 inches, and some truly jumbo, foot-long yellow perch.

"We've got about an hour left," said Gerard. "Want to try for northerns?"

"Any time. I'm a sucker for pike."

We scarcely had time to tie on wire leaders before John slowed the boat and cruised close to the mouth of a weed-fringed bay. Dangling from Gerard's rod tip was a red-and-white No. 2 Len Thompson spoon, the lodge's most popular pike lure. I dared to be different with a No. 2 Mepps Lusox spinner trailing a white, four-inch Mister Twister, its treble hook replaced by a large single with the barb crushed flat. As we cast in unison, Gerard again challenged, "Buck on the first pike?"

"You're on."

Near the end of our first drift, a 10-inch pike hit my spinner and managed to hook itself. When I hoisted it into the air, Gerard said, "You don't expect me to pay up for that little hammer handle, do you?"

"Of course! It's a fine specimen of *Esox lucius.*" I gripped the hook and slipped it free. "A bit small, perhaps, but certainly worth 10 cents an inch."

When we finally called it quits, the sun was rimming the treetops along the western horizon. The pike action had been sporadic, but even so we had landed and released a dozen fish of up to six pounds.

While unloading our boat at the dock, I pointed at our catch and asked Ron, "If this is your idea of slow fishing, what's it like when it's hot?"

"A lot faster paced. You can go to any of the falls and match this catch in a few minutes. In fact, if you just wanted a limit of five keepers, you could fill it in 15 minutes. But our guests are more interested in the experience than in filling limits, so everything goes back except the occasional big one. It's the only way they can stretch the day out, unless they want to fish for pike — and not many do."

The next two days saw continually changing weather dominated by low-flying grey clouds, occasional breaks of blue sky, gusting winds, periodic icy showers that verged on sleet, and one short but noisy thunderstorm that sent us scurrying for shore. Our dress consisted of warm boots, heavy clothing, caps with ear flaps, and rain slickers. It was cold, but our spirits remained high. And as Gerard pointed out, there was a distinct lack of biting insects.

Our guide for the remainder of our trip was Stanley McKenzie. Having lived in the area all of his life, he knew it thoroughly. Although he seldom took us to the same place twice, we usually located walleye with a minimum of searching, and seldom any deeper than 10 feet. They were eager to bite, for there were plenty of fish and the competition for food was aggressive. We released most, but a few were destined for our traditional shore lunch of golden-fried fillets, slab-cut potatoes, canned baked beans, bread and butter, and coffee — made in a one-gallon can, brought to a rolling boil from cold water. Black as molten tar, aromatic, and absolutely delicious, as only camp coffee can be.

Afternoons were devoted to pike, but the big ones proved scarce. Although the shallows teemed with them, the best we could muster was seven pounds. We knew the big pike were deeper, but our attempts at trolling large plugs and spoons along the steep drop-offs were thwarted by dense weed beds.

* * * *

Our final day at the lodge dawned bright and clear. Ron had a few winterizing projects to finish up, but said if we returned at 11 o'clock for lunch, we could fish the afternoon together.

George McKenzie, Ron's right-hand-man at the camp, and usually his fishing partner, was our guide for the morning. He suggested running upstream to Robertson Falls, an area we had not yet fished. It was pretty country, and each small bay produced pike averaging four or five pounds. After photographing the lacy white beauty of Robertson Falls, we started back, prospecting along the opposite side of the channel. By 10 o'clock we had shed our parkas and were basking in warm sunlight.

Things suddenly got exciting when Gerard's yellow-and-red Five of Diamonds was charged by the largest pike we had seen thus far. After missing the spoon it dove from sight, but Gerard quickly lowered his rod tip and jigged the lure up and down. Bang! The fight was on. It was a grand battle with some strong runs and lots of thrashing on the surface. Eventually George lifted the vanquished 10-pounder over the side for the obligatory photographs, then slipped it back into the water.

With lunch finished, we had about four hours before the Beaver arrived to pick us up. Ron and Gerard sped off, heading southeast through Cow Narrows, with George and me following in his slower boat. The narrow channel eventually opened into a wide bay, and far across its mirror-like calm we saw Ron's boat stopped near the shoreline. By the time we arrived, he had already been battling his behemoth for several minutes.

When weighed back at the lodge, Ron's pike did not quite pull the scale indicator to the 20-pound mark. However, for a lousy four ounces we agreed to lie about it.

An hour later, the sun was low and glowing fiery crimson on the horizon as our Beaver made a tight, growling turn above Beyond La Ronge Lodge, then banked southward. To the west, myriad lakes reflected the evening light, creating a scene of spectacular beauty in which the islands were like black silhouettes against a mirrored sea of deep, shimmering red. A memorable ending to an equally memorable trip. I chuckled, recalling Ron's parting words, "Next time come back during the summer and get into some fast-paced walleye fishing." I had just experienced some of the finest walleye action in my life, so I guess it depends on what you're used to.

CUBA ON THE FLY

British Columbia's Kamloops trout are the jumpingest fish, coho the fastest swimming, and summer-run steelhead a happy combination of both. Despite living in an area where all three are available, I have always had an urge to explore new locations and seek new species of fish. Thus, when Jack Simpson suggested a trip to Cuba for five days of saltwater fly-fishing, I started making plans. Jack had fished there several times, and spoke of world-class bonefish and tarpon on the Jardines de la Reina (Gardens of the Queen) Archipelago, about 50 miles off central Cuba's southern coast.

In mid-November, eight of us met in Toronto for the four-hour flight by Air Cubana to Cienfuegos. Jack, acting as tour leader, was the only one of our group with previous experience of fishing the Caribbean. After an overnight stay at the Rancho Luna Hotel in Cienfuegos, we boarded a 15-passenger, air-conditioned Mercedes Benz bus for the 125-mile trip east to the small fishing village of Jucaro. It was a pleasant trip through flatlands covered with sugar cane and groves of mangos, bananas and oranges, and the rolling, grassy plains were dotted with herds of cattle.

We arrived at Jucaro about 1 p.m., boarded the 65-foot "mother ship" *Practico 17*, and were off to sea a half-hour later. In tow were four 15-foot fibreglass boats with 30 h.p. outboards. The ship serving as quarters for our eight guides had departed earlier that day, also towing four boats.

Jack explained that we would reach the archipelago shortly before dark, then anchor overnight. After a 5:30 a.m. departure, we would arrive at the island chain's eastern end about 7:30. "That's the prime bonefish area at this time of year," he said. "We'll spend two days there, then start moving westward. When we finish up on Friday afternoon, Jucaro will only be three hours away."

That evening we dined on freshly-caught shrimp, rice, asparagus, fresh mango, and pineapple slices. It was the first of a series of excellent meals based on fresh seafood, including rock lobster, bonito, mangrove snapper, snook and barracuda.

When we reached our destination the following morning, each angler was assigned a guide and boat. My guide was Rafael Cebrera, a slim, wiry man with a ready smile and no English other than "left, right and centre," and the ability to count to 50 metres by fives (which would be used to alert me to cruising bonefish). My Spanish was limited to "*si, no, cerveza* (beer)," and "*gracias.*"

Within five minutes of leaving our ship, Rafael turned from the open Caribbean toward the mangroves. What appeared to be islands were actually dense groves of trees rooted to the ocean floor. Inside this ocean forest was a maze of large, open lagoons averaging one to two feet deep, joined by narrow, twisting channels. Once in the shallows, Rafael killed the outboard and tilted it up, then pushed us along with a 10-foot aluminum pole.

Bonefish are hunted by standing in the bow and searching the water's surface for movement, so amber- or brown-tinted polarized glasses are a must. The standard procedure was to cast out about 50 to 60 feet of line, then strip it in, coiling it carefully on the wide front seat that served as a casting platform. When bonefish were spotted, their direction of travel was determined, then the fly cast quickly ahead of them. Although bonefish are easily spooked, a well-presented fly stands a very good chance of being taken. When hooked, they don't jump, but streak away through the shallows at speeds approaching 30 miles an hour, often for 200 yards or more.

A brisk wind made spotting bonefish difficult, but Rafael, wearing neither hat nor glasses, pointed out occasional fish long before I saw them. I tried casting toward them, but as I was doing so against the wind, anything remotely approaching accuracy was impossible. When we quit at 11 a.m. for siesta, I had one nine-inch grey snapper to my credit.

Siesta is a common-sense practice that takes people out of the midday sun while it is directly overhead — usually from 11 until 1:30 or so. That afternoon I concentrated on photographing my companions hunting the open flats for bonefish. The wind had died, and at times we were surrounded by dozens of schools totalling hundreds, possibly thousands of fish. By evening, everyone with the exception of me had landed several bonefish, with the largest guesstimated at eight pounds.

My turn came the following morning in a shallow lagoon. After Rafael pointed out the tailing fish straight ahead, I tossed my line into a high back-cast, shooting it rearward to extend its length, then drove my 8-weight rod tip forward. The line shot smoothly and my tan-coloured shrimp pattern dropped cleanly in front of the advancing fish. After allowing the fly to sink for a few seconds, I started stripping in line and had an immediate hit.

I quickly discovered that what they say about the run of a bonefish being swift and sustained is true. However, instead of turning and running away from our boat, this one came straight at us, and while doing so passed on the outside of a four-foot-high mangrove stub jutting into the air about 40 feet in front of us. My reel was well into its Dacron backing when the fish streaked past, just beneath the surface. It was still accelerating when the leader parted. I reeled in to find that the external coating of my fly line looked as though it had been thoroughly scoured with coarse-grit sandpaper.

My next bonefish had the decency to turn and run toward open water. Although barely five pounds, it dragged an amazing amount of line from my reel before stopping about 150 yards away. Then it was simply a matter of working the exhausted fish back to the boat in order to release it.

That afternoon we trolled a large, blue-and-white, deer-hair streamer fly over the open flats at high speed, much like bucktailing for coho or chinook. Several two- and three-pound, deep-bodied jack crevalle were hooked, and fought with amazing strength for their size. Five small barracuda were also taken, none more than 20 inches long. They hit with the force and velocity of much larger fish, and fought strongly against my heavy 10-weight rod.

* * * *

The tallies that evening were good. Everyone had caught and released bonefish, a few tarpon had been "jumped" (a euphemism for hooked and lost), and various species of reef fish had fallen for our feathered offerings. All of the bonefish were released, but the jack crevalle, yellowtails and snappers went into the guides' larder. Simpson explained that they would also keep large barracuda unless told otherwise.

After the *Practico 17* was moved the following morning, it was anchored near a string of mangrove islands said to harbour the best tarpon fishing on Cuba's south coast. Tarpon are hunted in a fashion similar to bonefish, but usually in channels and lagoons with fairly brisk tidal flows. Unlike my slow start on bonefish, the tarpon came quickly to my rather garish-looking orange-and-yellow Stu Apt Tarpon Fly. Rafael selected a channel where, in less than an hour, I hooked five "baby" tarpon ranging from 2½ to four feet in length.

They were spectacular jumpers, often clearing the water by three or four feet, but after a half-dozen leaps their remaining fight consisted mainly of short-lived tugs of war until they were worked close enough to be released.

After siesta we headed for a large lagoon to troll for barracuda. As I paid out line, Rafael advanced the outboard's throttle until the boat was actually planing — probably about eight miles an hour. My fly had travelled scarcely 200 yards when the rod was nearly wrenched from my hand. A large barracuda greyhounded over the surface, leaped straight up twice in high jumps, then raced toward me so fast it was impossible to recover the bellied line. No problem. The fish streaked by as though it had been shot from a gun; this promptly took up the slack and ripped even more line from the reel, mangling most of my fingertips in the reel handles as they whirled into reverse. However, despite the violence and speed of the fight, it lasted barely three minutes. It should have taken longer, but as the barracuda again sped by the boat, Rafael reached out with his long-handled gaff and snatched it over the gunwale. This was a shock, then I recalled that during our briefing, Jack Simpson had explained that the guides would keep various reef fish and barracuda to take home as food for their families. Rafael had obviously decided this one was not going to get away.

The barracuda's body shape was similar to a pike or muskie, and its long, sharp, conical teeth looked very impressive. I guesstimated the toothy beast at 14 pounds, but Rafael upped it by two pounds.

Although my fly was shredded beyond belief, Rafael insisted I stick with it. It was good advice, for scarcely five minutes later it attracted a slightly larger barracuda, which fought even harder and longer than the first. After boating that fish I figured it at 16 pounds, but Rafael said 18. You have to love a guide like that.

Six days after we embarked, the mother ship finally docked at Jucaro. After goodbyes to our crew and guides, it was a tanned, happy group that boarded the bus for Cienfuegos and the flight back to Toronto. Except for me. About halfway back, I parted company with my friends at the Costa Sur Resort near Trinidad, for I had some writing assignments that needed attention. As none of them were related to fishing, I also parted company with my tackle, entrusting it to Jack Simpson.

TOURING CIENFUEGOS

As my Toronto-bound companions were leaving the Costa Sur Resort, I was busy meeting the two men with whom I would spend the next 10 days: Cubatur translator Tony Morfa, in his late twenties, and Turistaxi driver Angel "Jilly" McCatty, who looked about the same age but claimed to be 10 years older. After our preliminary greetings were dispensed with, Jilly announced in lilting English, "Hey, man, you look like Papa Hemingway."

"And you look like Harry Belafonte," I replied.

He laughed and waggled a finger at me. "You know, you aren't the first person to tell me that."

"Gee," Tony mused aloud, "I had no idea I would be travelling with such famous people."

"Well, at least we look like somebody," I said.

He nodded solemnly. "That's true. Some Americans once told me I looked like a movie actor, but I can't remember his name ... something about a sheriff or something."

I thought for a moment. "Sharif! Omar Sharif."

"That's it!" Tony seemed pleased that I knew the name, but then he shrugged. "I've never even seen a photograph of him, so I don't know if I really look like him or not."

"You do, but when he was much younger."

I turned to Jilly and asked, "How come you speak English like a Jamaican?"

He burst out laughing. "You have a good ear! My mother and father are from Jamaica, but they moved here before I was born. They always spoke English around home, so I learned it from them. And now I do the same thing with my son, Maxwell."

We had been together for only a few minutes, and already an easy camaraderie had formed. I decided it would be an interesting few days as Harry, Omar and Big Ernie explored central Cuba.

* * * *

The first leg of our journey was 150 km westward toward Playa Larga, at the northern end of the Bay of Pigs. As our amazingly well-maintained 1975 Toyota followed the ribbon of asphalt threading through the Sierra Escambray foothills, I marvelled at the beauty and lush crops surrounding us. Tony slipped easily into his tour guide's role and provided a running commentary on what we were seeing: fields of malanga (taro), a large apiary with hundreds of bee hives, teak trees, royal palms, coconut palms, and Cuban bamboo, which, given enough water, grows one centimetre per day. Pig farms were common, as were large herds of "F-1" cattle, a heat-resistant cross between the Holstein and Zebu breeds, which was developed by Ramon Castro Ruz (Fidel's brother).

A large complex of buildings was identified as apartments for farm workers. Tony said the guarantee of a job and a comfortable apartment encourages many young people from the area to take up farming and related activities after completing their education.

Each bridge crossing a stream or backwater had a few anglers draped over the railings, fishing with handlines. A few were adult men, probably on days off work, but most were pre-teen boys. We stopped occasionally and asked the universal question: "Catching any?" Everyone was friendly and eager to show what they had caught. Most of the fish were deep-bodied tilapia up to 10 inches long, with a smattering of juvenile largemouth bass, few more than eight inches long.

We stopped near a large hotel, then walked along a pathway to a wharf on Cienfuegos Bay, where five men and a young boy were fishing with handlines. Most of their catch consisted of small, shiner-like fish about three to six inches long, but one fellow — obviously the king fisherman — had two jack crevalle weighing about three pounds apiece, and a small octopus that might have spanned two feet.

We made our way back up to the car, then drove to the hotel parking lot. Although it catered to tourists, there was a small cantina in one corner for staff and locals. We seated ourselves at a table and the bartender approached to take our order. Jilly still had some driving to do, so he settled for an orange soft drink. Tony and I asked for *cerveza*, the excellent local beer that comes in tall, unmarked, brown bottles. The bartender shook his head and informed us there was no *cerveza*. Tony pointed toward a young couple seated at a nearby table, each with a tall brown bottle before them. "What are they drinking?" he asked.

"My last two *cerveza.*"

I suggested we have a Cuba Libre. Again, the bartender shook his head. "We have no Cuba Libres, senor."

"Do you have five-year-old Cuban rum?" Tony asked.

"*Si*, of course."

"Do you have cola?"

"*Si.*"

"We will have two drinks of rum and one cola."

After the bartender dropped off our drinks and returned to the bar, Tony followed him and asked, "Do you have any fresh lime?"

"*Si.*" He held up a fresh, uncut lime.

"May I have two pieces, please?"

The bartender carefully quartered the lime, then offered each of the two pieces on the point of his knife. Tony thanked him, returned to our table and handed me one piece. We squeezed the juice into our glasses, then sat back to enjoy our Cuba Libres.

After we left Cienfuegos, the terrain started levelling as we passed orange groves, mango plantations, and fields of sugar cane. Tony again switched into his tour guide spiel and explained the importance of sugar to the Cuban economy: "Sugar cane is a perennial that grows for five years. In addition to granulated sugar, molasses and our justifiably world-famous Cuban rum, the stalks provide paper, cardboard, and chipboard used for building material. The residue provides fuel for steam boilers, and the leaves are mixed with molasses for cattle food."

I switched off my mini-recorder, then asked him to repeat what he had just said. He did it word for word.

IN HEMINGWAY'S FOOTSTEPS

(AUTHOR'S COMPLAINT: The remarks began soon after I started growing a beard in the late 1970s. As grey stubble formed on my jowls, the lady to whom I had been married for nearly a quarter century at the time, looked at me from across the table with a puzzled expression, then finally said, "You look like Ernest Hemingway." I assumed she was trying to be funny, but as my beard flourished, so did comments about the resemblance. Now the truth is, my only likeness to that illustrious writer is the grey beard. If I dyed it red or black, or shaved it off, I would revert to the anonymity of being old whazzisname. I know this for a fact, because as you read on, you will discover that I have it on possibly the best authority in the world that I don't look the least bit like Hemingway....)

No foreigner is as revered in Cuba as Ernest Hemingway, the Nobel Prize-winning author who ended his life in 1961. Several locations in Havana are designated as official memorials to him, including two of his favourite restaurants: La Bodeguita del Medio and La Floridita. Others are room 511 at the Ambos Mundos Hotel, where Hemingway stayed while writing *The Old Man and the Sea*, and the Hemingway Museum, his estate in San Francisco de Paula, 12 km south of the city.

I knew about these places from a previous trip to Havana, and had visited all but the hotel. While planning my return trip to Cuba, I decided to try visiting as many of the memorial sites as possible to take photographs. Sort of an "in the footsteps of Hemingway" project, for whatever might evolve from it.

After arriving in Havana and getting settled in at the Hotel Panamericano, Tony and I spent our first evening relaxing and discussing the next three days, and Jilly sneaked off to visit his wife, Aidita, and son, Maxwell. The following morning, the three of us set out to visit a few places which Tony, his tour guide instincts getting the best of him, insisted I had to see. Having done our duty, around noon we headed for La Bodeguita del Medio for a refreshing mojita, followed by a lunch of roast pork, rice and beans. Simple fare, but memorable for its wonderful taste.

Next on our agenda was La Floridita. It was early afternoon when we arrived, but business was booming. As Tony had suggested we drive 10 km out of town to the village of Cojimar, we stayed only long enough for me to scribble some notes and shoot a few photographs.

The Ambos Mundos Hotel was our next stop. As we walked into the lobby I saw it was obviously old — a bit worn and shabby, but clean. Tony asked the receptionist if we could speak with the manager.

"He is with two salesmen right now, but he should only be a few minutes."

Tony glanced at me and shrugged. "If it's a 'few minutes' in Cuban time we might be here a long time."

I returned his shrug. "So — I've still got three days."

The hotel was not large, only five storeys high, but it had obviously once been quite magnificent. Like most old buildings in Havana, it was in need of repairs; unlike the majority it was actually getting them. Outside, there was scaffolding along one wall, and inside were signs of the construction workers' equipment. However, it being Sunday, no one was working.

Less than five minutes had passed when the manager's office door opened and three people emerged. The salesmen, identified by leather briefcases, said their goodbyes and departed, whereupon the receptionist informed the manager he had more visitors. He approached and introduced himself as Roberto Lafita. Tony told him I was a journalist from Canada, and explained that I would like to visit the room where Ernest Hemingway usually stayed whenever he was in Havana. "Certainly," Lafita replied. "Excuse me while I get my keys."

As the manager disappeared into his office, Tony turned to me, his mouth open in an exaggerated expression of shock. "I can't believe this!"

"What?"

"He said 'yes' just like that! No hesitation, no argument, no explanation about why it's not possible to see the room at this particular time ... nothing. I tell you, Bob, it's not the Cuban way! We have to discuss these things to death."

Lafita returned and ushered us toward the elevator, an ancient cage of ornamental ironwork that creaked and groaned its way to the top floor. We were led down the hallway to the end, where he unlocked the door to room 511. The first thing I noticed was the huge, black typewriter perched on a small table.

"This is the room where Hemingway stayed," said Lafita. "Most of the furnishings are authentic. The bed is original, and that table, but not the typewriter. We could not get the original he used to write *The Old Man and the Sea*, but this is an identical machine. The problem with this being a hotel is that over the years some of the furnishings were replaced, and there were some upgrades, like a new toilet in the bathroom."

There was an assortment of Spanish books and magazines on one of the dressers. Lafita explained they were representative of the period. "We have tried to recreate the room as it was when Senor Hemingway stayed here, to make it as similar as possible." He slowly shook his head, then smiled ruefully. "It is too bad they did not know he would become so famous — they could have started preserving things much earlier. But we have done the best we could."

I told him it was fine, just fine ... and I meant it sincerely.

* * * *

When Tony first suggested we visit Cojimar, the name sounded vaguely familiar but I could not place it. It was not until we were actually there that things fell into place, albeit vaguely, and I recalled mention of the tiny fishing village in my favourite Hemingway book, a collection of articles and dispatches titled *By-line: Ernest Hemingway*, published in 1967.

The 10-km trip from downtown Havana took only a few minutes, during which time Tony briefly consulted his "travel guide's bible" and informed me that Hemingway had often visited Cojimar to write, fish for giant blue marlin, and carouse with his Cuban friends. He became well-known and loved by the villagers, and when news of his death was received, they took it upon themselves to erect a monument honouring his memory. It proved quite an undertaking for people who had little monetary wealth, but they accomplished their goal by stripping the brass fittings from their fishing boats to provide metal for a life-sized bronze bust. Completed in 1962, the bust is surrounded by six tall pillars of stone which dominate the village square. Fittingly, the monument is positioned so Hemingway's likeness gazes out over the Florida Strait he so loved to fish.

We parked on the street separating the cobblestone square from the sea wall overlooking the harbour, then set about photographing and videotaping the monument. While we were thus engaged, a young woman emerged from a nearby building, watched us for a moment, then walked across the square to introduce herself as Maritza Rodriguez, manager of the Cojimar Tourism Office. Tony explained what we were doing, whereupon she offered to show us around the village. As we strolled along the sea wall, Maritza explained that of Hemingway's many friends in Cojimar, the closest had been Gregorio Fuentes, who had served as the mate on his boat. "Would you like to meet him?" she asked.

"You mean he's still alive?" I said.

"Yes. He's very old now, but he welcomes visitors."

I was truly surprised, for I recognized the name from some of Hemingway's accounts of fishing in Cuba. "I would love to meet him! Lead the way."

With Maritza giving directions, Jilly drove carefully through the narrow, cobblestone streets until we reached a small, faded-blue house with a red tile roof. Sitting just inside the open front door was Gregorio Fuentes. He rose slowly from the wrought-iron rocking chair, and at Maritza's greeting beckoned for us to enter. He was neatly dressed in slacks and a long-sleeved shirt, and wore a white baseball cap with a leaping marlin embroidered on the crown. He looked frail, but as we shook hands his grip was firm.

After the introductions had been made, Maritza asked him in Spanish, "Does he look familiar?"

Fuentes peered at me momentarily. "No."

"Does he not look like Ernesto?" she said.

Fuentes shook his head. "No," he repeated firmly. "Not at all."

Maritza turned to us and quietly whispered, "His eyes are not very good now."

Fuentes raised his right hand and shook his finger at her. "My eyesight is better than you give me credit for, young lady — and so is my hearing."

Hemingway's presence dominated the small living room. On the rear wall hung a large, limited edition print depicting the author and Fuentes. In the painting's background, they were shown hauling a large marlin over the transom of *Pilar*, Hemingway's boat. A large black-and-white photograph of Hemingway hung on another wall, above two easy chairs and a sofa that had seen better days. Although timeworn, the room was comfortable: a covered television set in one corner, a spray of colourful plastic flowers jutting from a vase, a wooden rocking chair, plus two more of wrought iron.

Our host excused himself and left the room. He returned with a large book, written in Spanish and filled with black-and-white pictures, which chronicled Hemingway's life. While leafing through its pages, Fuentes said he was a year older than Hemingway. "I was born on July 11th, 1898, and he was born on July 21st, 1899."

He told us they first met in 1928, when Fuentes was captain of his own fishing boat. During one trip, a strong northeast gale forced him and his crew to take shelter at Dry Tortugas, a small island west of the Florida Keys. Hemingway and his mate were already there, riding out the storm. Shortly after Fuentes dropped anchor, Hemingway came alongside to see if they could buy some fresh onions. Fuentes invited them aboard for a drink, which led to several more, then he and Hemingway took their rum and rowed ashore to explore the ruins of an old Spanish fort. The storm eventually lessened, but Hemingway said it was still too much for his boat to handle. He asked Fuentes to take him to Key West, about 100 km east. Fuentes replied, "But you are American and I am Cuban. You know that according to law I'm not allowed to do that."

Hemingway laughed and said, "But you can't just leave us here, Gregorio — there's nothing here."

Fuentes thought it over then said, "Okay. Let's have another drink, then I'll take you to an island that has a lighthouse and you can send a message by radio."

Although the water was still fairly rough, their trip to the lighthouse was uneventful. After they had landed there, the lighthouse keeper notified the U.S. Coast Guard, and a boat was sent to pick up Hemingway. As Fuentes prepared to leave, the grateful writer shook his hand and said, "We'll meet again some day in Cuba."

Hemingway was true to his word, for from then on, whenever his travels took him to Havana he visited Fuentes. In 1938, after

Hemingway returned from the Spanish Civil War, he hired Fuentes as the *Pilar*'s mate.

"I enjoyed travelling with Hemingway," said Fuentes. "I have never met anyone like him in my life — he had a special power, an ability to communicate with people no matter where they came from or what language they spoke. Usually, when Hemingway and his wife, Mary, arrived in Cojimar, they went shopping and stocked up on groceries for the boat. He usually wrote during the mornings, so his wife would go fishing with me near Cayo Paraiso, which is not far offshore.

"We would return around noon, and Hemingway would join us for lunch aboard the *Pilar.* Then he would say, 'Okay, Gregorio, let's go somewhere.' Sometimes we had a plan before we left the wharf, other times we decided after we left. His favourite fish was marlin, and the largest he ever caught weighed 1,542 pounds." Fuentes paused, then slowly repeated the weight and smiled. "Hard to believe, isn't it?"

I asked Fuentes if he might have been Hemingway's role model for *The Old Man and the Sea.* He shook his head. "No. *The Old Man and the Sea* was based on several of the fishermen who lived here, but not any particular one. One time when we were heading west toward Pinar del Rio, we saw an old man and a young boy in a boat. The old man was struggling with a big blue marlin, and he must have been at it for quite a while because he was very tired. When he saw us, he started swearing at us because he thought we wanted to steal his fish. Hemingway told me to move our boat away, then sent me below to fill a couple of bags with food.

"We went back in close to the fishermen and threw the food down to them, then we left. That's what gave him the idea, but that's all. His inspiration for the fisherman came from many of the fishermen here in Cojimar that he knew personally."

Fuentes pointed toward me. "One evening Hemingway was sitting here in this room — in that chair. He had finished writing the book but didn't know what to call it. I said, 'Well, there was the old man and there was the sea....' Hemingway said, 'That's it! We've got it! *The Old Man and the Sea!*'"

Fuentes said that in 1935, Hemingway had been foiled in his attempt buy a house in Cojimar. "The owner was a Spaniard named

Boaba. He wanted one million dollars for his house, and Hemingway said, 'I've never seen that much money in my life!' "

Now faded and run down, the huge structure of stone and concrete looks out over La Terraza Restaurant, where Hemingway used to meet his friends to eat, drink and party. He eventually purchased the large, colonial-style house in San Francisco de Paula, which now serves as the Hemingway Museum.

Over two hours later, as we prepared to leave, Fuentes ducked into an adjoining room and returned with his guest book. I noted the first entries had been written in 1990, indicating other books were probably full and stored away. All but a few pages were filled with dedications, comments, addresses and the signatures of people from around the world. Over half were in Spanish, for Cuba is popular with tourists from South America, Mexico and Spain. There were also many comments in English, but oddly enough, most had been written by visitors from Japan. After we had signed his book, Fuentes shook my hand and asked, "When will you come back to Cuba?"

"Soon, I hope."

"Good! When you do, come to visit me and we'll talk some more."

I assured him that I would. As our car pulled away from the tiny house, I touched my fingertips to my forehead in salute to the old man standing in the doorway. When he promptly returned my salute I had to chuckle — there was definitely nothing wrong with his eyesight. And I finally had indisputable proof — with witnesses — that I do not resemble Ernest Hemingway.

QUEBEC REDS

It started over a drink on New Year's Day when Andy said, "I phoned my Uncle Clem in Baie Comeau last night. He said he found a spot last June that was swarming with Quebec reds. What say we go after them this spring?"

Andy wasn't talking about large gatherings of Quebec residents with communist leanings, but lake-dwelling Arctic char that don crimson mantles when they enter tributary streams to spawn. Being a West Coaster, I had never seen, let alone caught one, so I was easily talked into making plans for shortly after ice-out. Like most anglers, I adhere to the adage about distant pastures being greener. Never mind that a river or lake on my doorstep is teeming with hungry fish, there is always a spot in some other county, province, state or country that just might be better.

It was mid-June when we left Ottawa in Andy's car, his 14-foot Sportspal lashed to the roof rack, the back seat and trunk laden with our tackle, spare clothing, and extra rations of insect repellent. "Uncle Clem said there won't be any mosquitoes this time of year," Andy said. "The blackflies keep them thinned out."

At Riviere-du-Loup we crossed the St. Lawrence River by ferry to Tadoussac, then continued up the north shore. When we arrived in Baie Comeau, about 500 new miles were registered on the car's odometer, but those Quebec reds were still well over 100 miles farther north.

It was midday when we finally arrived at a picturesque little lake. Clem's camp consisted of a small, spartan, one-roomed cabin, plus a 20-foot trailer equipped with a propane stove and refrigerator, even running water from a nearby holding tank.

Clem and his wife had led the way in their heavily-laden station wagon. After helping them unload the equipment they required to set up camp for the summer, Andy and I moved our gear into the cabin, slathered on liberal coatings of insect repellent, then dug out our wide-brimmed hats and head nets. It was too late to set out for Clem's Quebec red hotspot, so we launched Andy's canoe in the lake to try for a few brook trout. We fished hard, mostly with tiny weighted spinners, and caught four small trout. Emphasis on small — like eight inches.

Following breakfast the next morning, Andy and I paddled nearly a mile up the lake, to where a blazed tree marked a portage to the next lake. The well-used trail was crooked and steep, and mostly up. We took turns carrying the lightweight canoe over the quarter-mile hump, much of it verging on perpendicular.

The second lake was quite narrow, and also a mile or so long. Another lake lay beyond, but it was only a few feet higher in elevation. It was in the small creek between the two lakes that, Clem assured us, we would find the bottom carpeted with Quebec reds.

Andy spotted them shortly after we beached the canoe. "There they are!" Sure enough, a small school of scarlet fish was clustered in the deep water across from us. Andy opened the bail of his ultralight spinning reel and flicked a small weighted spinner above the fish. Nothing. He tried again, then changed lures and continued casting, but to no avail.

I left Andy and strolled up the trail. The bottom of each pocket and run of deep water was lined with red fish, but I continued walking until I found a bend where the creek changed course, so the deep water was on my side. I lay down on the bank and edged forward slowly, in order to peer down at the fish without startling them.

I was still there when Andy finally approached. "I can't believe it," he announced. "I've tried every lure I've got, and they're not the least bit interested in any of them."

"Get down and crawl up here for a look," I said.

Andy peeked over the bank, then cursed and started pounding his fist on the ground. The sudden vibrations sent hundreds of fish darting into shallow water, which gave us an even better look at their large scales and underslung mouths. "Meunier rouge!" he exclaimed angrily. "We drove over 600 miles to catch red suckers!"

"No, no, Andy," I admonished. "They're Quebec red suckers."

A SECRET PLACE

Everyone should have a secret place, even adults supposedly beyond the stage of playing games. Mine, thus far shared with no one, is a small tract of still-wild lowland near the city. The land is marginal: rocks, tall grass, willow thickets, scrub alder. I suppose some folks might consider it useless, but I know better. There is protective cover for grouse, and the tangled mat of grass is criss-crossed with bunny runs.

Grosbeaks, warblers and wrens share the thick foliage, and occasionally I hear the grating call of a ubiquitous crow, or see a soaring hawk silhouetted against the sky. There are foxes, skunks and raccoons, even a few mink and deer. I never see them, for they are secretive and shy, but their signs are in the soft damp earth bordering the creek that meanders through the glen. Its waters support a small population of brook trout. As befits their surroundings they are tiny fish, averaging six or seven inches long. Once, however, I caught a deep-bodied male fully 10 inches long, a handsome, hook-jawed fellow with a back so deep green it was nearly black, in sharp contrast to the cream-coloured spots, flecked here and there with brilliant dots of blue-rimmed crimson, which patterned his sides.

I seldom have qualms about taking fish for food, especially those as tasty as brookies — but I have never kept one from that Lilliputian stream. Without lifting the little char from the water, I slipped my barbless hook from his jaw, then watched him dart for the far side of the pool. Since then, on those all-too-rare occasions when I visit the little creek, my rod stays in the car. After all, I have jousted with the king himself; why bother with commoners?

Because of the spot's proximity to the city, I suppose it's only a matter of time before the land developers move in. I shudder at thoughts of arriving someday to find brightly-coloured plastic streamers tied to various tree branches. They will be reminders that progress is every bit as relentless as time, taxes and death.

When it happens, the bird songs will be drowned out by the growling roar of heavy equipment; the prints of paws and cloven hooves will blend with the scarred earth left by tractors and bull-dozers. The creek, far too serpentine to remain, will be straightened and made more "efficient." There will be no room for riffles or pools or overhanging banks, for they have nothing to do with the important task of moving water from point A to point B. Possibly it will disappear entirely, routed through a concrete pipe buried beneath the surface. In either case, the brook trout, too, will disappear.

In the meantime, whenever time permits, I visit my secret place. It is pleasant and relaxing, the air still clean and smelling of trees and grass and creek mud. I sneak away and leave behind a world of ever-increasing madness; forget about senseless wars fought in the name of religion and ethnic origin. There, for a while at least, I can pretend there are no poisons being dumped into our waters, no noxious fumes pouring into the air, no acid rain falling over the countryside, no mindless expansion of asphalt and concrete into our marshlands and valleys. Childish? I suppose so. Making believe doesn't solve problems — or make them go away — but it provides my senses with a much-needed respite, which makes facing hard facts just a wee bit easier.

It's a nice spot, my secret place. There, my only worry is progress....

THE MECHANICS OF FISHING

Whenever Mert includes me in plans for a fishing trip, the outcome can be seriously life-threatening. Take the incident involving a canoe, Class IV rapids, large rocks, a high waterfall, and Mert asleep in the bow — which accounts for my prematurely grey hair. Unlike instant spasms of terror which are over in a nanosecond, our hurtling descent through that horrific, raging maelstrom lasted over a minute. The sudden rush of blood draining from my face apparently created a vacuum that sucked the colour out through my hair roots.

Not all of Mert's escapades are scary. Some are merely frustrating, uncomfortable, boring, or a combination of all three. During my recent visit to Toronto, Mert met me at the airport. Later, while careening down the traffic-jammed 401, he announced that in the morning we were meeting Jock Sampson at his cottage on the Trent River, northeast of the city. "They're getting some real big small-mouths," he said, releasing the steering wheel to spread his hands, indicating what would surely be a new world-record bass. "Monsters!" he added as our pickup wandered into the adjoining lane, right toward the long trailer of a big cross-country rig with several dozen extremely large wheels. Mert laughed as he steered back into our lane. "And they're as thick as all that grey hair standing straight up on your head."

Jock's cottage is on a shallow, lake-like stretch rimmed with cat-tails, lily pads, and other cottages. It was my first time there, and I was pleased to see that his boat was an open, 18-foot bow rider with a wide trihedral hull, the sort three could fish from in comfort.

After warming up the big outboard motor, we cast off and Jock headed toward mid-channel, then turned upstream. Even at half throttle the 100 h.p. outboard moved us along at a brisk clip, until it suddenly quit about three miles upstream. Abruptly. No cough, rattle or hesitation — one moment purring smoothly, the next deathly silent.

I am noted for my mechanical knowledge. Whenever an outboard quits on me, I simply shake the gas tank, ensuring there is fuel; check both fuel line fittings; squeeze the rubber pump a few times, then try restarting. I then determine whether it makes more sense to paddle ashore, or simply wait for a tow. I used to remove the cover and look at the little glass jar to see if there was fuel in it, then wiggle the thick black wire between the big part in the middle and the small white thing on top. However, I could never get the cover back on, so this stage was eliminated.

My companions being experienced boaters, I felt confident they would quickly resolve the problem. A half-hour later we were finally under way, discussing how difficult it is to paddle an 18-foot bow rider with a wide trihedral hull; how a wind blowing upstream totally nullifies any assistance provided by the current's downstream flow; how barren of boats that popular stretch of water becomes at certain times of the day; and mostly how hot the sun was.

We eventually reached Jock's dock — dog tired, hot, sweaty, tongue-hanging-out-thirsty, and, of course, fishless. While Mert and I unloaded our equipment, Jock casually twisted the ignition key before removing it. The outboard roared into life, then settled down to a smooth idle. Jock's lips moved as he gazed heavenward, but I doubt that he was praying. He switched off the motor, then joined us as slowly, wordlessly, we dragged ourselves up to the cottage. Where we discovered Mert had left our beer in the open back of his pickup. It, too, had spent all day in the hot sun.

WHAT FRIENDS ARE FOR

The problem with Hotchkiss is that he loves fishing but hates spending money on it, or on anything else for that matter. Minor purchases are made only after days of agonizing indecision, while major expenditures, like buying an overpriced bottle of single malt scotch, leave him bordering on terminal depression. Which is why much of his equipment comes from flea-markets, yard sales and bargain basements. Then there is the stuff he makes himself — like his Personal Flotation Device fashioned from a fluorescent orange hunting vest and aluminum beer cans filled with granulated foam plastic. He placed the cans in rows between the lining and outer shell, then stitched between them with heavy thread. It is truly ugly, but he swears it keeps him afloat. I hope never to be around if he has to use it.

His chest waders are so heavily patched that the knees barely bend. Hotch puts them on by sitting on the tailgate of his pickup, inserting both feet, then sliding down into the boots. He can walk only by rolling from side to side, and should he trip and fall, the only possible way he can get up is by crawling to the nearest tree or rock, then hauling himself erect. It's a pathetic sight, believe me.

Despite his parsimonious nature, Hotch is a good friend and a great fishing companion. Except when we use his boat, which happens at least once whenever I visit him in Ontario. Hotch claims *Titanic II* is of "composite construction," which sounds like something fashioned from Kevlar, ABS or similar space-age materials. Not true. "Compost construction" is a more fitting description, it being moulded from something that looks suspiciously like it might once have resided in a bovine digestive tract. Whatever the material, its rupture-inducing dry weight doubles after 30 minutes in the water. Annual coats of whichever house paint happens to be on sale are applied over previous layers, which add to its weight, but are probably instrumental in holding it together and slowing down the seepage.

Titanic II is 12 feet long, four feet wide, and barely higher on the sides than most duck boats. Its low bow is squared off, punt style, which causes the slightest ripple to splash upward and spray over the top, which is where I always sit.

Our most recent outing on Lake Simcoe was more or less typical: Hotch spent 15 minutes starting his outboard, a procedure complicated by the rope breaking twice. I have never determined his motor's country of origin. It looks like an early prototype for an industrial-sized mechanical eggbeater, but the undecipherable writing stamped on its corroded metal surface consists of strange symbols instead of recognizable letters.

We spent the afternoon trolling on Hawkstone Shoal, the *Titanic II* trying to submerge beneath oncoming waves whenever we travelled upwind, and me bailing furiously to prevent it. This left Hotch free to catch several smallmouth bass, which he released, and a 10-pound lake trout, which he kept. I managed to fish whenever we sped quickly downwind, then Hotch would turn upwind again for that long, slow, wet trip along the shoal. Even so, I released a few scrappy bass, so it was a very good day. Sure, I was cold and wet and my back hurt from bending over to bail, but despite *Titanic II*'s best efforts we didn't sink.

Later, with the aroma of baking lake trout wafting from the kitchen, we discussed life in general over tots of Highland nectar. At one point Hotch said, "Jonesy, there's one thing I have never been able to understand — how in hell do you manage to keep coming up with new things to write about?"

I studied him over the rim of my glass. "Experience," I replied. "Being there. And the truth is Hotch, old buddy, I simply couldn't do it without friends like you."